Venture Capital Networks

Venture Capital Networks

A Multilevel Perspective

Cristiano Bellavitis

Contributors:
Igor Filatotchev
Vangelis Souitaris
Dzidziso Samuel Kamuriwo
Joost Rietveld

 BUSINESS EXPERT PRESS

Venture Capital Networks: A Multi-Level Perspective
Copyright © Business Expert Press, LLC, 2018.

First published in 2018 by
Business Expert Press, LLC
222 East 46th Street, New York, NY 10017
www.businessexpertpress.com

ISBN-13: 978-1-63157-984-4 (paperback)
ISBN-13: 978-1-63157-985-1 (e-book)

Business Expert Press Finance and Financial Management Collection

Collection ISSN: 2331-0049 (print)
Collection ISSN: 2331-0057 (electronic)

Cover and interior design by S4Carlisle Publishing Services
Chennai, India

First edition: 2018

10 9 8 7 6 5 4 3 2 1

Printed in the United States of America.

Abstract

In the venture capital (VC) industry, firms often co-invest with other peers in syndicated deals. The process of syndication is a form of investment alliance that generates networks of VC firms and start-up companies. Despite the prominent role played by syndicates, extant entrepreneurship literature found contradicting evidence on the relationship between the practice of syndication and the performance of both the start-up and the investors. In fact, our understanding of the circumstances under which syndicates have the potential to boost performance, rather than hamper them, is still limited. Previous literature suggested that syndicates improve the access to resources for both the entrepreneurs and the VC partners. However, syndicates, as opposed to solo investments, carry agency costs such as free riding and conflicts of interests among co-investors.

I investigate the role of syndicates on performance building upon network and alliance literature. Recent studies show that syndicates, networks, and alliances have the potential to be both an asset and a liability for the focal actor. This applies to the amount of connections that a firm has, the structure of its network, or the composition of the alliance. I apply a contingency perspective to investigate the boundary conditions under which syndication exerts a positive rather than a negative effect on performance. I test theoretical claims at three levels of analysis: at the start-up level, at the VC investors' level, and the syndicate level.

In order to fulfill these research goals, this book covers multiple levels of analysis and syndicate's characteristics. The three chapters each cover a different factor likely to impact syndicate's performance. In Chapter 1, I investigate the effect of the portfolio companies' network on the performance of the start-up. In Chapter 2, I study the impact of the focal VC firms' network structure on the performance of the VC investor. In Chapter 3, I research the impact of the syndicates' composition on the performance of the syndicates. Thus, taking different angles and unit of analyses, I provide a holistic picture of conditions under which syndicates prove to be advantageous to the focal actor.

First, in the VC industry networks are formed by co-investing together. Although the VC literature acknowledged the importance of networks among VC investors, our understanding of the importance of networks for the portfolio companies is still limited. The first chapter fills this gap. I study the impact of being connected with other companies within a given portfolio on the performance of each start-up. Furthermore, most network literature took a "structuralist" approach, forgoing the differences between ties. Therefore, I complement this literature by showing that not all portfolio ties are equal. I differentiate between *intra-* and *extra-industry* ties between portfolio companies and show that not all ties are beneficial to the performance of the focal start-up in the same fashion.

Second, I move the analysis to the VC firm level. Although the VC literature investigated how VCs form networks by co-investing together and, in turn, how this affects performance, it has overlooked the fact that networks of VC firms differ in structure, and different network structures offer different performance benefits. I aim to fill this gap by studying the effect of a cohesive and a structural holes network on the performance of the focal VC. In doing so, I also contribute to the debate between cohesion and structural holes that, although highly relevant, is still unresolved. I show that, hitherto, extant literature treated the focal firm exogenously, focusing the attention on the network externalities. Considering that different network structures offer different resources, I show that the benefits of a particular network structure are contingent on the resources already in possession of the focal VC firm.

Third, I take the syndicate as a unit of analysis. Previous VC literature pointed out that VCs repeatedly transact with each other, thus engendering familiarity. Yet, the impact of familiarity among syndicate partners on the performance of the syndicate has not been tested yet. Building upon the alliance literature that stressed the importance of alliance familiarity, I show that the level of familiarity embedded in a co-investment alliance has a curvilinear effect on the performance of the alliance. Furthermore, I show that the effect of familiarity on syndicate performance is contingent on the nature of familiarity, namely, familiarity arising from successful as opposed to non-successful previous interactions, as well as contextual factors such as the age of the start-up and the development stage of the VC industry.

Keywords

Alliance; cohesion; network; repeated collaborations; start-ups; structural hole; syndicate; technology; venture capital.

Contents

Acknowledgments

The author and contributors gratefully acknowledge the helpful comments from Robert Hoskisson, Martin Kilduff, Curt Moore, Keith Brouthers, Hans Frankort, Rayan Krause, Benjamin Hallen, Elena Casprini, Mike Wright, Santi Furnari, Kaizad Doctor, Orkun Saka, Andre Silva, and Beth Bechky for their valuable comments. We are also grateful to our industry informants Omar Sati, Sam Guo, Giuseppe Folonari, Rogan Angelini-Hurll, Hussein Kanji, and Brian Karlson. Versions of these chapters have been presented to various seminars and conferences. We are grateful to seminar participants at Imperial College Business School (London, UK), Rice University (Houston, US), Texas Christian University (Fort Worth, US), McGill University (Montreal, Canada), City University of Hong Kong (Hong Kong), Higher School of Economics (Moscow, Russia), Luiss Guido Carli University (Rome, Italy), and University of Sussex (UK). We are also indebted to participants at EGOS (2015, Athens), EURAM (2015, Warsaw), and SMS (2016, Rome) conferences. Finally, we would also like to thank Katy Brown for her ongoing support. The usual disclaimers apply.

Introduction

"Venture capitalists are committed to funding America's most innovative entrepreneurs, working closely with them to transform breakthrough ideas into emerging growth companies that drive U.S. job creation and economic growth."

—National Venture Capital Association, NVCA 2017

Entrepreneurship is the backbone of a developed economy and a robust venture capital (VC) industry is key to sustain entrepreneurship and economic development (Avnimelech and Teubal 2006; Bellavitis et al. 2017; Ferrary and Granovetter 2009; Wright et al. 2009). In 2016, U.S. VC firms invested $71B whereas their UK counterpart poured into the British economy $1.3B (in 2015).[1] However, U.S. and UK investments in venture-backed companies represent approximately 0.1 percent of the national GDP each year, these start-ups have a proportionally much stronger impact on the economy. For example, U.S. and UK[2] VC-backed companies employ, respectively, 11 percent and 17 percent of the national private sector workforce. Furthermore, U.S. VC-backed start-ups in 2013 generated revenues equal to 21 percent of the U.S. GDP.

These results are not the mere consequence of better selection of start-ups. A British Venture Capital Association (BVCA 2002) survey found that nearly half of the portfolio companies reported that their levels of employment had been higher due to venture backing. VCs are usually

---

[1]Particular care has been taken to ensure comparability of the statistics reported. Yet, some challenges arose. First, the definition of VC slightly differs between the U.S. and the EU/UK VC industry. Where possible, I tried to make the two systems comparable including in the UK statistics only venture capital related statistics which are similar to the definition of the U.S. VC. Yet, this was not always possible as in some cases is difficult to disentangle the UK VC from UK private equity investments. Second, some UK statistics are only available at the EU aggregate level and it was not possible to disentangle the country contribution.

[2]The UK employment statistic is derived from EU statistics.

the only form of capital available to innovative companies that would otherwise find it impossible to develop and sustain their businesses. A survey conducted by the European Venture Capital Association (EVCA 2002) found that 95 percent of portfolio companies could not have existed or would have developed more slowly without a VC investment; 72 percent of seed/start-up companies stated that they would have never come into existence without the contribution of VC; and almost 60 percent said that the company would not exist today without the contribution of VC.

The benefits of VC investments are also reflected in strong capital market activity. In 2013, 81 U.S. VC-backed firms went through an IPO raising $11.1B. These companies represent 36 percent of the companies listing and 20 percent of the amount raised in the U.S. markets. Furthermore, in 2013, in the U. S. 376 firms went through M&A activity worth approximately $16.5B. On the other hand, VC/PE-backed IPOs represent 36 percent of European IPO deal numbers, whereas M&A deals totaled $4.25B (EY, Q1 2014; 2012 statistics).

VC-backed companies have been a powerful tool for economic development, but some of them radically changed the way that individuals live their lives. In recent years, U.S. and UK VC firms funded some of the most successful companies worldwide such as Facebook, Cisco, Microsoft, Starbucks, Snapchat, Twitter, Linkedin, Mendeley, Last.fm, FedEx, Ebay, Google, Amazon, Skype, Apple, and many others.

Most of these success stories are not the result of a lonely effort. Both entrepreneurs and VCs require networks and partnerships to guide and nurture ventures toward a bright future. In order to establish networks and tap into valuable resources held by multiple investors, VC investments tend to be syndicated (Wright and Lockett 2003). Precisely, Dimov and Milanov (2010) found that 72.8 percent of U.S. VC investments between 1980 and 2004 have been syndicated. Due to the relevance of the VC industry for the economy as a whole, and the preponderance of the practice of syndication, this phenomenon received considerable attention in various literatures such as finance (e.g., Hochberg et al. 2007, 2010), strategy (e.g., Echols and Tsai 2005), sociology (Ma et al. 2013), and entrepreneurship (e.g., Lockett et al. 2006). Yet, we are still unclear on the conditions under which a syndicated VC investment leads to better performance of both the start-up and the investors.

Some studies advocated a positive impact on performance due to networking benefits (Bellavitis et al. 2014; Manigart et al. 2006; Bygrave 1988; Hochberg et al. 2007; Sorenson and Stuart 2001), access to network resources (Bellavitis et al. 2017; Gargiulo and Benassi 2000; Hite and Hesterly 2001; Stuart et al. 1999), risk diversification (Manigart et al. 2006), increased access to deal flow, better selection, improved monitoring, and value-adding activities (Brander et al. 2002; Bygrave 1987, 1988; Lerner 1994). Therefore, it was generally assumed that syndicates lead to higher performance than solo investments, facilitating a successful exit through an IPO (Cumming and Walz 2010). Brander et al. (2002) found that solo investments have an average rate of return between 15 percent and 20 percent whereas syndicated investments achieved between 34.8 percent and 39 percent per year.

However, recent studies found evidence of the detrimental or non-significant effect of syndication on performance (Meuleman et al. 2009; Hege et al. 2006; Dimov and De Clercq 2007). This can be explained by the fact that, although syndicates have the potential to improve the performance of both the VCs and the start-ups, they are also associated with significant agency risks and coordination costs (Filatotchev et al. 2006; Steier and Greenwood 1995; Wright and Lockett 2003).

Thus, a better understanding of the conditions under which syndicates provide benefits that outweigh their costs is needed, and this is the first aim of this book. I do so by departing from the assumption of homogeneity of syndicates and focal firms that so far most VC studies took. Previous studies focused on the impact on performance by various social capital characteristics such as the centrality (e.g., Hochberg et al. 2007) or status (Stuart et al. 1999) arising from syndication. Other studies simply counted the number of investors or used a dummy to code for syndicated versus non-syndicated deals (e.g., Tian 2011). However, although these approaches are straightforward, they overlook three important contextualizations: the type of connections that the focal firm establishes, the surrounding network structure, and the composition of the syndicate.

In complementing previous VC studies, I show that a syndicate is a co-investment alliance that generates a network of firms. I argue that syndicates can be both an asset and a liability depending on (a) the type of connections generated by syndicated deals, (b) the structure of the network arisen from syndication, and (c) the composition of the syndicate. These three factors significantly shape the trade-offs posed by syndication and are therefore able to pinpoint the boundaries under which syndication ought to be preferred to solo investing at the start-up, VC, and syndicate level. In order to support my theoretical claims, I thoroughly investigate the advantages and disadvantages of syndicates in different geographical contexts, with different levels of analysis and from different theoretical lenses.

In particular, in Chapter 1, I build upon the work of Lorrain and White (1971) that called for more research adopting a contingency perspective in which the categorization of the networks is based on tie attributes rather than structural measures. Distinguishing between connections in the same or in other industries, I investigate how different ties lead the focal investee company to better performance, namely, the achievement of an IPO or an M&A event. This chapter not only contributes to the VC literature but also to the network debate between "structuralist" (e.g., Coleman 1988) and "attributist" (e.g., Peng and Luo 2000) and shows that studying network centrality is not sufficient to fully explain the performance benefits of certain networks, but rather network attributes ought to be considered.

In Chapter 2, I posit that different syndicates lead to different network structures that, in turn, offer different performance benefits to the focal investor. Furthermore, previous network research has focused predominantly on the network's ability to supply relevant resources to the focal firm (e.g., Dahlander and Frederiksen 2011), and it overlooked differences between firms in terms of their idiosyncratic resource needs (Oh et al. 2004). I show that the VC firm's resources shape the additional resources needed by the firm, and potentially accessible through its network. I investigate the effect of the stock of resources controlled by the focal VC firm, either internally or externally, on the benefits derived from a particular network structure (i.e., cohesive network or structural holes). I research the effect of network structures on the achievement of successful exits (IPO/M&A). This chapter contributes not only to the VC literature but also to the overall network field by showing that different firms experience different benefits from their network structure. Furthermore, it contributes to the debate between cohesion (Coleman 1988) and structural holes (Burt 1992) by showing that both structures provide advantages but under different resource endowments.

In Chapter 3, I focus on the role of the social capital generated by repeated interactions (i.e., familiarity). Previous VC papers acknowledged the repeatedness of VC interactions but, hitherto, the impact on performance has not been tested. Therefore, I show that the performance of the focal VC is affected not only by its centrality or status generated by co-investments, but also by the familiarity with its partners. This chapter contributes to the VC and alliance literature at large. Considering that previous alliance studies found contradicting results on the benefits of familiarity, I try to reconcile these competing findings proposing that familiarity increases trust but at the same time reduces the resource diversity of the syndicate. I show under what conditions syndicate familiarity is beneficial to the performance of the group of investors. Furthermore, I answer the call for more research (Lunnan and Haugland 2008: 545) to broaden our understanding of "why some alliances fail while others perform well over time" that still "remains one of the most exciting and unexplored areas" of alliance research (Gulati 1998: 306) and I show that familiarity among partners has a strong impact on the performance of the co-investment alliance.

I empirically test my hypotheses in the VC industry both in the UK and in the U.S. In line with previous network (Hochberg et al. 2007) and alliance studies (Chung et al. 2000), I operationalize networks from syndicated investments. I try to use complementary perspectives. In fact, while in Chapter 1, I focus the analyses around the network of the portfolio companies connected through common investors, in Chapter 2, I take the perspective of the focal VC company, and in Chapter 3, the syndicate is the focal point. In addition, while the first two chapters benefit from comprehensive data on VC investments in the UK, in Chapter 3, I use the U.S. data. My quantitative analyses are enriched with interviews with VC practitioners.

Declaration

The chapter titled "The Effects of *Intra-* and *Extra-Industry* Networks on Performance of Venture Capital Portfolio Firms" has been published in the journal *Managerial and Decision Economics*. The chapter titled "The Impact of Investment Networks on Venture Capital Firm Performance: A Contingency Framework" has been published in the *British Journal of Management*.

CHAPTER 1

The Effects of *Intra-* and *Extra-Industry* Networks on Performance of Venture Capital Portfolio Firms

This study examines the influence of *intra-* and *extra-industry* networks on firm performance by using data on 1,264 UK venture capital (VC)–backed start-up companies. The ventures' network was operationalized by connecting together the various portfolio companies sharing the same investor. Regression results show that the venture's network has a strong impact on firm's success. Yet, whereas *extra-industry* ties are directly and positively linked to the likelihood of the venture to reach a successful exit, *intra-industry* ties exert a negative impact on companies' performances. However, interaction effects show that once a firm establishes a sufficient number of *extra-industry* ties, it is able to profit from the network in its industry of operation. Overall, these findings show that an optimal balance of ties is achieved through a diverse set of connections incorporating both intra- and extra-industry ties.

1.1   Introduction

Although a venture's network may facilitate the pursuit of new opportunities, provide access to innovative knowledge, and hence enhance performance, it is increasingly recognized as not only an asset but also a potential liability that constrains the firms' operations and is costly to maintain (e.g., Baden-Fuller et al. 2011; Brass et al. 2004; Gargiulo and

Benassi 2000; Stam and Elfring 2008). A better understanding of the conditions under which a venture's network enhances a firm's performance may thus require a contingency perspective in which the categorization of the networks is based on tie attributes rather than structural measures (Lorrain and White 1971). As pointed out by various scholars (e.g., Dahlander and Frederiksen 2011: 1002; Gulati 1995: 645; Lavie 2006; Maurer and Ebers 2006), while much work has focused on the structural attributes of the firm's networks, surprisingly few studies have examined how heterogeneous ties, in particular intra- and extra-industry connections, impact the firms' success. The limited empirical evidence that exists suggests that, although networks may enhance performance of entrepreneurial firms, not all ties do so equally (Peng and Luo 2000). Thus, identifying the contingency conditions under which particular networks enhance or constrain venture's success represents an important research agenda (Lee et al. 2001).

In this study, we aim to contribute to previous network literature by studying how network capital that is embedded in the intra- and extra-industry ties of entrepreneurial ventures impacts the firm's success. In the economics and entrepreneurship literature, a network is seen as invaluable for the entrepreneur because it provides access to resources, contacts, and opportunities (Ahuja 2000; Aldrich and Martinez 2001; Batjargal 2003; Baum and Oliver 1991; Birley 1985; Bruderl and Preisendorfer 1998; Combes et al. 2005; Dimov and De Clercq 2006; Knack and Keefer 1997; McEvily and Zaheer 1999; Podolny and Baron 1997; Stuart et al. 1999). Networks also play a pivotal role in enabling actors to discover opportunities (Burt 1992), perceive, and exploit them (Companys and Mullen 2007). However, some researchers highlight the cost of managing networks and propose a cost–benefit trade-off associated with networks. Gargiulo and Benassi (2000), for example, conclude that "like the tightrope walker who maintains balance by constant movements of his balancing pole, the successful individual or organization in today's business environment may have to continuously balance the trade-off between safe (e.g., *intra-industry*) and flexible networks (e.g., *extra-industry*)." Contributing to recent efforts to integrate this apparently opposing views, we try to reconcile these perspectives (e.g., Oh et al. 2004; Stam and Elfring

2008) building on the premise that network capital has contingent value (Ahuja 2000).[1]

Therefore, we propose that optimal firm performance results from a specific balance of intra- and extra-industry ties. Since simultaneously establishing these two sets of ties may involve significant trade-offs, it is relevant to understand whether they are complementary or duplicative (Stam and Elfring 2008). We argue that both types of networks provide ventures with access to distinct resources (Geletkanycz and Hambrick 1997), and we show that the value of such access is maximized when a firm combines the two types of ties in a certain proportion. Once the venture departs from this optimal combination of intra- and extra-industry ties, its chances of being successful drop. However, if we consider the ties separately, it appears that *extra-industry* ties are more beneficial to a firm's success than *intra-industry* connections.[2] We argue that the positive effect of *extra-industry* ties is predominantly related to the knowledge and resource diversity to which these ties give access to. On the other hand, *intra-industry* ties offer resources that the venture may already possess, and with a lack of *extra-industry* ties, the venture will not be able to take advantage of a brokerage position between the two "worlds."

Using a combination of secondary data, hand-collected firm-level variables, and primary sources on networks of VC-backed ventures in the UK, this research specifically examines how a firm's intra- and extra-industry VC portfolio network centrality contributes to the success of the firm. Addressing recent calls for "more complex, multidimensional models that investigate the interactions between different types of social capital conduits" (Oh et al. 2004: 870), in particular differentiating between intra- and extra-industry ties (Gulati 1995a: 645), we aim to

---

[1] Ahuja (2000) argues that the nature and content of the ties, the type of outcome being studied, and the broader network structure within which a tie is embedded are all likely to influence the value of a tie. We use the nature and content of the ties as a contingency.

[2] Intra- and extra-industry ties represent a measure of network composition which refers to the types of actors defined by their stable traits, features or resource endowments (Phelps, 2010; Wasserman & Faust, 1994) whereas tie strength or weakness refers to the content of the tie i.e., the extent to which the actors refer to each other.

identify the configuration of network ties that maximizes the contribution of networks to ventures' success.

1.2   Theory and Hypotheses

Networks can be defined both as an entrepreneur's attempt to mobilize personal contacts in order to profit from entrepreneurial opportunities (Granovetter 1985) and as a firm's effort to cooperate with others in order to obtain and sustain a competitive advantage (Peng and Luo 2000). Brass et al. (2004) define a network as a set of nodes and the ties representing some relationships, or lack of relationships, between the nodes (individuals, work units, or organizations). Network structure relates to the pattern of relationships that exist among a set of actors, while network composition refers to the types of actors defined by their stable traits, features, or resource endowments (Phelps 2010; Wasserman and Faust 1994). The content of the relationships represented by the ties can vary widely, and it is limited only by a researcher's imagination (Brass et al. 2004). Specifically, we define the network as the actual and potential resources available to a firm through its network of relationships (Nahapiet and Ghoshal 1998) established by VC-backed ventures within the portfolio of each VC investing in the firm.

Building on recent research (e.g., Dahlander and Frederiksen 2011; Geletkanycz and Hambrick 1997), we focus our attention on the ties' attributes rather than structural measures. Our focus on network attributes is based on a premise that, although prior work has examined the core discussion related to networks of entrepreneurs (e.g., McEvily and Zaheer 1999) and the structural differences of ties (e.g., Stam and Elfring 2008), this literature lacks systematic research differentiating the resources accessible through different types of ties, therefore acknowledging the heterogeneity of the connections. This study specifically examines two important dimensions of a firm's network: (1) *intra-industry* network ties and (2) *extra-industry* ties. Following the differentiation between "internal" and "external" social capital (Adler and Kwon 2002), our approach builds on the notion that intra- and extra-industry ties provide a focal firm with access to distinct social capital resources, in line with Geletkanycz and Hambrick (1997) and Stam and Elfring (2008).

However, our study departs from Geletkanycz and Hambrick (1997) and Stam and Elfring (2008) on various important dimensions. First, these authors study the impact of ties at the executives' level, rather than at the firms' level; second, their sample is related to publicly traded firms while our sample is composed of young firms operating in rapidly changing environments. Third, methodologically they assume the existence of external ties while we adopt specific and longitudinal measures that allow us to precisely identify the amount of external connections and their nature. Hence, to the best of our knowledge, this study is the first which specifically studies the impact of intra- and extra-industry ties on entrepreneurial ventures' success.

1.2.1 Entrepreneurial Ventures' Success

In this study, we look at the effect of two types of ties, intra- and extra-industry, on firm's success. In this section, we explain how we define success. Entrepreneurial ventures, especially in their early years, are usually cash flow negative or have very limited profits. Many VCs argue that valuing a start-up is more an art than a science but the industry agrees that the exit is the ultimate acknowledgment of the start-up market value and therefore its success. Therefore, considering that the main successful [exit] routes considered in the literature are Initial Public Offerings (IPO) and trade sales (Manigart and Wright 2013: 56), in this study, we consider the company exit as our measure of success.

1.2.2 The Role of Intra- and Extra-industry Ties

Previous studies suggest that ventures with central network positions enjoy several advantages that contribute to higher performances (Brass et al. 2004). Being highly connected allows a firm to learn about new market conditions, strategies of competitors, and partnership opportunities (Powell et al. 1996) and have access to alternative providers of valuable resources (Tsai 2001). However, different ties offer different benefits and each tie has a particular trade-off between costs and benefits (Baden-Fuller et al. 2011).

In rapidly changing environments, such as the one in which entrepreneurial ventures are embedded in, firms increase their performances by focusing on ties that offer nonduplicative resources in order to gain new information and knowledge (Christensen and Raynor 2003; Duysters 1996). For instance, biotechnology start-ups with networks providing access to diverse information have higher revenue growth (Baum et al. 2000). *Cosmopolitans*—entities that are connected with different networks or industries—are more likely to innovate, and are therefore potentially more successful (Dahlander and Frederiksen 2011). Furthermore, resource heterogeneity accessed through connections is an important source of success (Hagedoorn and Schakenraad 1994; Penrose 1959; Prahalad and Hamel 1990; Ring and Van de Ven 1994).

In this light, we posit that *extra-industry* ties, connections that span outside the main industry of operations of the focal firm, lead entrepreneurial ventures to succeed not only because they offer access to a diverse knowledge base and heterogeneous resources, but also because they help the firm to gain power and potential for brokerage opportunities. Considering that ventures should develop new routines, competencies, and technologies and that *extra-industry* ties facilitate access to complementary resources that are not available within the industry boundaries (Stam and Elgring 2008), and therefore stimulate exposure to a diversity of approaches, perspectives, and ideas that are not well established in the focal industry (Hargadon 2002), allowing the focal firm to "bring together new combinations of productive factors" (Low and Abrahamson 1997: 443), *extra-industry* ties are very valuable for new ventures. In sum, *extra-industry* ties are more likely to lead the firm to success by functioning as a scanning device that allow entrepreneurial firms to detect new trends and asymmetries in a market faster than firms lacking such connections.

In addition, *extra-industry* ties provide power, allowing a firm to diversify its ties across different industries and therefore avoid the control by few others who control critical resource exchanges (Pfeffer and Salancik 1978:131). Similarly, diversifying ties offers the possibility to broker contacts in different industries that would probably otherwise be disconnected. Therefore a firm that spans contacts across industries is less likely to be dependent on each of these contacts, but rather other firms are dependent on the firm itself (Kotter 1979).

The advantages provided by *extra-industry* ties are not without costs. In fact, this type of ties involves higher risks and coordination costs (Burt

1992). However, we argue that these two disadvantages are mitigated by the presence of a common investor that helps to reduce transaction and coordination costs through its intermediation (Hsu 2006).

Symmetrically, the main advantage of *intra-industry* ties is that they offer a cohesive environment with a common ground of behavioral rules (Coleman 1988) and therefore low risk and coordination costs. Furthermore, *intra-industry* ties provide industry legitimacy, and reduce uncertainty regarding the firm's quality. However, VCs already play a strong role providing legitimacy (Stuart et al. 1999), information about the quality of the firm (Sapienza et al. 1996), and an environment where failure to comply with the network rules is coupled with severe punishment (Burt and Knez 1995).[3]

In addition, being dependent on one main industry for connections and resources is likely to increase the firm's competition over the resources; in fact competition tends to arise in organizations that are functionally equivalent, in that they are attempting to produce similar products and services for similar markets (Pfeffer and Nowak 1976).

Therefore, from the previous discussion we hypothesize that starting from the assumption that entrepreneurial ventures should favor nonduplicative connections, *extra-industry* connections will be more beneficial to the firm's success.

H1: *The VC-backed venture's success will be positively (negatively) associated with extra-industry (intra-industry) ties.*

1.2.3 The Optimal Combination of Intra- and Extra-industry Ties

Recent work indicates that usually network forms are not inherently at odds, but rather that ties may benefit the firm but under different conditions (Rowley et al. 2000). For instance, Baum et al. (2000) show that increasing the number of connections without considering partner's diversity can create inefficient configurations that generate less diverse information and capabilities at greater costs than a smaller, nonduplicative

---

[3] As concluded by Gargiulo and Benassi (2000), one would expect that actors would favor the safety provided by a dense network in situations where the risk of opportunism and the cost of malfeasance are high and a network rich in structural holes (e.g., *extra-industry* ties) in situation where trust is not an issue.

set. Accordingly, various scholars (e.g., Burt 2000; Provan et al. 2007; Reagans and McEvily 2003; Reagans and Zuckerman 2001; Soda et al. 2004; Tiwana 2008) demonstrate that an optimal network may be the one that combines different elements such as cohesion and structural holes or strong and weak ties.

We argue that the effect of *intra-industry* ties is positively moderated by the presence of *extra-industry* ties and vice versa. Stam and Elfring (2008) argue that *extra-industry* ties broaden the knowledge base of a highly central firm and increase its capacity to appreciate, recombine, and apply the knowledge that is accessible through its *intra-industry* ties (Cohen and Levinthal 1990). Put simply, ventures with high *intra-industry* centrality and extensive *extra-industry* ties occupy a unique brokering position that enhances their capability to recognize information asymmetries in the market and connect seemingly unrelated facts into novel combinations (Burt 2000; Hargadon 2002). Exposure to new ideas and resources via *extra-industry* ties may outweigh any conformist pressures coming from *intra-industry* ties (Perry-Smith and Shalley 2003). In addition, being directly tied to other fields makes highly central firms less dependent on industry peers for access to new knowledge and resources (Pfeffer and Salancik 1978). These ventures are able to verify and triangulate information received from competitors and VCs with information received through bridging ties, thereby enhancing their access to high-quality information that facilitates the pursuit of innovative, high-risk–high-reward opportunities (Stam and Elfring 2008) that are necessary to achieve an outstanding success. Hence, we argue that a firm has to carefully balance its portfolio of ties in order to combine intra- and extra-industry ties.

H2a: Intra- and extra-industry *ties complement each other in enhancing the firm's success.*

H2b: *There is an optimal network portfolio composed of a set of* intra- and extra-industry *ties which leads to the firm's success.*

1.3   Methods

1.3.1 Research Setting

The empirical context of this study is the UK VC industry during the period 1995–2011. The VC industry is an interesting context because it involves the financing of new or radically changing firms which are different in many important ways to mature, established companies quoted on the stock markets (Wright and Robbie 1998). VCs usually operate in private finance markets that are often characterized by a low liquidity and information frictions (Bengtsson and Hand 2011). In this context, networks prove to be useful in reducing information asymmetries, enhancing performance through access to crucial resources, and conferring legitimacy. Although networks may play important roles in overcoming such knowledge and legitimacy challenges, most research has looked at established industries (Aldrich and Fiol 1994; Geletkanycz and Hambrick 1997). The UK market has been chosen because, although it is the biggest in Europe (EVCA 2010) and the third most attractive worldwide for this type of investments (IESE 2010), it has received considerably lower attention than the U.S. market (with research by Abell and Nisar 2007; Chiplin et al. 1997; Filatotchev et al. 2006; Manigart and Wright 2014; being notable exceptions).

1.3.2 Research Design and Data Collection

We collected data from multiple sources to establish the validity of our measures. First, we conducted a qualitative study using field interviews with portfolio firms and VCs, archival data, and a literature review to explore possible impact of portfolio companies on each other.[4] Based on theoretical and qualitative evidence, we argue that there are strong links between VC portfolio companies. Companies with a common VC investor may exchange experiences and knowledge, rely on the economies of scale in dealings with suppliers, and have cross company directorships which may impact their operations. The importance of this type of networks is highlighted by entrepreneurs and investors such as InvestorLab, Kleiner Perkins Caufield and Byers, Rocket Internet, Intel Capital, First Round, as well as by scholars (e.g., Hsu 2006; Lindsey 2008; Stuart et al. 1999).

---

[4] This approach has been proven to be fruitful in the network literature by other scholars such as Gulati (1995), Powell et al. (2005), Soda et al. (2004), Stam and Elfrig (2008), and Uzzi (1996). For example, Gulati (1995) uses interviews in 8 firms to confirm the relevance of his research, and Uzzi (1996) refines his framework based on interviews and fieldwork.

We started with interviewing three VC-backed entrepreneurs and three VCs and gathered secondary data using VC websites among other secondary sources.[5] Online resources taken from VC websites (e.g., iGlobe, First Round Capital, Intel Capital, Rocket Internet, Kleiner Perkins Caufield, and Byers-KPCB) illustrate the existence and importance of portfolio–company ties. For instance, KPCB, one of the leading U.S. VCs, emphasizes on its website[6]: "Entrepreneurs gain access to our matched portfolio of companies and associations with global business leaders. These relationships are the foundation for strategic alliances, partnership opportunities and the sharing of insights to help build new ventures faster, broader and with less risk." Furthermore, our interviewees explained that two practices are common in the industry in order to foster networking among portfolio companies: CEO/CFO mailing lists and CEO summits.

In addition, various scholars have demonstrated that common third parties (e.g., common VC investor) serve as an incentive to display cooperative image (Burt and Knez 1995; Gargiulo and Benassi 2000; Gulati 1995; Hsu 2006; Lindsey 2008; Stuart et al. 1999; Uzzi 1997).

Furthermore, Powell et al. (1996) and Barringer and Harrison (2002) suggest that collaborations in high-tech industries typically reflect more than just a formal contractual exchange and are often stipulated with social contracts rather than legal agreements. Therefore, based on theoretical and practical evidence, we posit that VCs can create an environment where collaborations between their portfolio companies can blossom, but these collaborations are often informal and not legally binding.

Once we established the existence of these links among portfolio companies, we gathered VC investment data through the Thomson One Banker database. The database contains the same information as Venture Expert which has been extensively used in the VC literature (Chaline

---

[5] Although our main quantitative analyses and data collection are UK-based, we conducted interviews also with non-UK-based VCs and entrepreneurs and extensively reviewed online resources worldwide. We believe that this procedure does not confound our findings as the western VC standards are common throughout the different markets.

[6] http://www.kpcb.com , quote retrieved on 28th of July 2011.

et al. 2012; Gompers 1995; Hochberg et al. 2007; Lerner 1994). We included UK-based venture companies that received the first VC investment between 1995 and 2008 with records of investments up to the end of 2011. Following the approach used by Hochberg et al. (2007), we did not include companies that received their first investment after the 2008 to allow ventures sufficient time to successfully exploit their potential, or eventually fail. On the other hand, the analysis starts in 1995 because prior to this year the Venture One database does not provide a comprehensive coverage of the UK market.

In line with Manigart and Wright (2014), we focused our attention on "young growth oriented venture capital-backed companies" that therefore received investment from seed to later stage, therefore excluding buyouts, real estate investments, and generally private equity deals. For additional refinement, borrowing from Zahra (1996), we defined new ventures as firms that have been in existence for eight years or less at the time of investment. We also did not consider companies that received investments exclusively from "undisclosed investors" or "individual investors" because this does not allow us to locate the venture within a VC network. The final data set contains 1,264 VC-backed companies, 5,344 VC deals made by 733 VC firms. After additional data collection and manipulation, we created a panel of precise network measures for each venture in each year.

1.3.3 Network Construction

The database has been initially rearranged to create a matrix of 1,264 companies per 733 VCs per 17 years, totaling 15.7 million data points. Venture Expert divides the portfolio companies according to their status: previously or currently VC backed. For previously VC-backed companies, we hand collected a date and type of exit through multiple database sources such as Zephyr, SDC Platinum, MergerMarket, and Venture One. However, when the venture was listed as "Currently VC backed" and there was no evidence of exit or bankruptcy from other databases, we assumed that the VC is still a shareholder in the company. Finally, if the company's exit was coded as "went public," "acquisition," "merger," and at the same time it was not VC backed, an exit date has been calculated in relation to the stage of the company following Gorman and Sahlman (1989).[7]

Subsequently, in line with our field research and our theoretical underpinnings, we redesigned the network as portfolio–company to portfolio–company matrix. This generated a matrix with 1,264 companies and 17 years totaling around 27 million data points. Connecting portfolio companies with each other through a common link with a VC is similar to the network validated by Venkatraman and Lee (2004) that connected game developers through video-games consoles.

1.3.4 Measures

Performance

As previously mentioned, the company trade-sale or IPO is a strong acknowledgment by the market about the company value. Hence, in line with the VC literature, our dependent variable of success is represented by a VC exit (e.g., Hochberg et al. 2007). This performance measure is considered to be the most appropriate because, due to the high levels of technological and R&D intensity of the firms in our sample, accounting performance measures may be misleading, especially during early stages. Therefore, an exit is a clear and objective way to assess the entrepreneurial firm's performance and the success of the VC investments (Cumming 2007). IPOs and acquisitions are widely regarded as the best exit outcomes for both the company and the VC (Abell and Nisar 2007; Cumming et al. 2006; Cumming and MacIntosh 2003; Gompers and Lerner 1999; Manigart and Wright 2014; Megginson and Weiss 1991).[8] With regard to acquisitions, it has to be noted that this type of exit is not always financially rewarding but we argue that it is a good proxy for value

---

[7] We assumed that early stage investors reduce the amount of time devoted to companies in the seed stages after 8 years, in the early stages after 7 years, for companies in the balanced and later stages after 3 years.

[8] An IPO is not strictly an exit at the time of the public offering since some of the VCs' equity may be held after an IPO within a lock-up period. However, an IPO still allows VCs to cash in a significant portion of their pre-IPO equity and get their portfolio firm recognized by public market investors as a successful venture.

for both the company and the shareholders. Therefore, in order to test our hypotheses, we used a dummy that takes the value of 1 if the venture has been acquired, merged, or went through an IPO in a given year.[9]

Intra- and Extra-industry Ties

In order to test our hypotheses, we developed two measures that represent the amount of ties that each venture has in (a) the industry of operations (*intra-industry ties*) and (b) in external industries (*extra-industry ties*). The two variables are constructed taking into consideration six macro industries identified by the Thomson One database: Computer-related Communication and Media, Non-High Technology, Biotechnology, Semiconductors/Other Electrical and electronics, and Medical/Health/ Life Sciences. The choice of the above classification comes from two main reasons: (a) there is a generally even distribution of companies among the six categories compared to more fine-grained segments and (b) using more precise industry measures reduces the likelihood of a firm to have a connection with a company in the same industry; in fact, even using only six industries, a single company on average has less than 1 connection in the same industry and 2.5 connections in unrelated industries each year. Based on this industry classification, we developed two distinct matrices for each year for each venture representing the ties among the various portfolio companies with a common investor. Therefore, if two companies share the same investor in a given year, they belong to the same network. In addition, the ties have been divided in intra- and extra-industry based on whether the connections are in the same or in different industries with regard to the focal company. Hence, each venture in any given year of its life has two set of connections: intra- and extra-industry connections. We then created an interaction effect by multiplying the intra- and extra-industry network variables in order to test our hypothesis 2a.

---

[9] For example, if the firm is in the network from 2000 but went through an IPO in 2003, our performance variable will have 0s from 2000 to 2002, and a 1 in 2003. Within our dataset, 30% of the companies have been acquired, merged, or went through an IPO while 7.5% failed. The ratio between write-offs and successful exits is in line with the one identified by the British Venture Capital Association for the last available years at the time of this study (4 years).

In addition, to test hypothesis 2b, we include two different but related measures: Concentration of ties and proportion of ties.

Concentration of Ties

We include a concentration index that helps us to better understand the best combination of ties. We create an index based on the following Herfindahl formula, where S represents the proportion of ties in each network; we created yearly concentration measures of ties. Therefore if a firm in a given year has only *intra-* or *extra-industry* ties, rather than a combination of the two, will have a concentration measure of 1. Similarly, if it has 50 percent ties in each of the networks, this index will have a value of 0.5.

$$H = \sum_{i=1}^{N} S_i^2$$

Proportion of Ties

Finally, in order to shed additional light on the optimal concentration of ties as suggested in hypothesis 2b, we calculated the proportion of intra- and extra-industry *ties* based on the following equation, where C is the concentration of ties both for I (*intra-industry ties*) and E (*extra-industry ties*):

$$C_I = \frac{I}{I + E} \quad \text{and} \quad C_E = \frac{E}{I + E}$$

Furthermore, we tested the robustness of our findings with alternative measures of networks such as *betweenness*, *Bonacich power*, and *eigenvector* generated for both types of networks (for a detailed discussion of these measures, see Bonacich 1987; Borgatti et al. 2002; Freeman 1977; Hochberg et al. 2007).

Control Variables

To ensure the robustness of our findings and to rule out alternative explanations, we include a number of controls. Brander et al. (2002) find that syndication is associated with higher returns. Therefore, we include the *Number of co-investors* in each venture over its life.[10] Kaplan and Schoar (2005) show that returns are persistent across a sequence of funds managed by the same VC firm. Hence it can happen that older VCs are more reputable and therefore invest in more successful ventures within their portfolio and this could create a similar bias to the one previously mentioned (Podolny 2001). Therefore, we include the *VC Experience* which is represented by the logarithm of the total number of companies invested in to date by the lead investor.[11] In addition, we also include dummies that classify the *Stage of the VC* fund investing in the company (i.e., Early stage, Balanced Stage, Later Stage, Other). Furthermore, we check whether the lead VC fund is *UK based* (dummy with value 1 if UK based) and whether the fund and the portfolio–company have their headquarters in the *Same city* (dummy with value 1 if in the same city). These measures are likely to account for the potential networking spillovers generated by the VC proximity that it is known to be relevant in the VC investments (Cumming and Dai 2010; Sorenson and Stuart 2001). Furthermore, to control for market conditions, we gathered from the World Federation of Exchanges the yearly net amount of listed companies on the London Stock Exchange (*LSE*)[12]. Control measures related to the ventures include dummies for the *Industry* of operations, the *Age at financing*, and the dynamic *Age*. For example, if a venture is 12 months old at the time of the VC investment in 2005, the

---

[10] To control for the effect of syndication, we follow the definition of Lockett, Ucbasaran, and Butler (2006) that defined an equity syndicate as two or more venture capital firms taking an equity stake in an investment for a joint payoff, either in the same investment round or at different points in time (Brander et al. 2002).

[11] This measure is calculated for each venture from the inception of the lead VC to the time of the first investment in the portfolio company. An option to include VC measures considering the lead investor only is suggested by Gorman and Sahlman (1989). They theorize that when VCs play a lead investor role, they devote much more time than non-lead or late-stage investors, and they invest in every round with a bigger amount of capital overall. Hence, we identified a lead investor as the first VC to invest in the company. We do not have data about the investment for a reasonable number of companies to check the effective size of the investment. In unreported tests we also controlled for VC age and results are consistent. However, due to collinearity issues, we could not include both measures simultaneously.

[12] This measure represents the new listings minus the de-listings.

Age at financing measure will be 12 all over the company's life. Differently, the dynamic *Age* will be 12 in 2005, 24 in 2006, 36 in 2007, and so forth.

1.3.5 Analytical Methods

In order to test our hypotheses we run a longitudinal logistic regression with random effects that tests the impact of our predictors on the likelihood of a venture to have a successful exit. The fixed-effect model using dummy variables to control for firm or time differences is not appropriate since some explanatory variables are time-invariant (Gulati 1995: 652; Hausman and Taylor 1981).[13] Furthermore, as reported by Lincoln et al. (1996), OLS gives inefficient estimates of slopes and (negatively) biased estimates of standard errors with pooled cross-section/time series data because it fails to take into account the error components common to the same firms in different periods and different firms in the same periods. Therefore, the random-effects model applied to a logistic regression is the most appropriate estimation technique. Furthermore, we standardized our network measures of around the Z-score to avoid high inter-item correlations among the interaction terms (Gao et al. 2010). Therefore the variables Intra- and Extra-industry ties have been standardized and after this procedure, we interacted the variables following Friedrich (1982).

1.4   Results

Tables 1.1 and 1.2 report the descriptive statistics and correlations. Within our sample, more than 74 percent of the firms had the lead investor based in UK and 20 percent of the companies were located in the same city of their investor. With regard to the fund stage, the sample is approximately evenly spread within the three stages: early (42 percent), balanced (28 percent), and later (21 percent), with just a few companies in "other" stage (7 percent).[14] The most represented industry sectors are "Computer

---

[13] As a robustness test, we run a model with fixed effects including only time varying measures. The results of this test are explained in the next sections.

[14] This measure is related to the stage of the VC fund, but it can be considered a proxy for the stage of the company as well. This measure is conceptually different from the Age since not all companies need the same time to reach the same stage of development.

Software and Services" and "Internet Specific" which represent almost half of the firms. Furthermore, the average firm received the first VC investment 31 months after the inception from 3 VCs co-investing together, with a maximum of 22 firms co-investing in Oxagen Ltd. The average age of the company in our panel is 5.7 years. With regard to the networks' size, we can see that the results are highly skewed. In fact, even though the average is 1 and 2.4 for intra- and extra-industry connections respectively, the maximum amount of connections is 39 and 83. Finally, on average, 56 new companies have been listed on the London Stock Exchange every year.

Table 1.1 Descriptive statistics

Variable	Mean	SD
Successful exit	0.0511	0.220
Intra-industry ties	0.9320	3.052
Extra-industry ties	2.4371	7.315
Co-investors	3.0694	2.782
Age at financing	31.2573	23.521
VC/Venture=City	0.1957	0.397
UK fund	0.7466	0.435
Early stage	0.4216	0.494
Balanced stage	0.2871	0.452
Later stage	0.2179	0.413
Other stage	0.0734	0.261
Computer SW	0.2046	0.403
Internet	0.2082	0.406
Communication	0.0903	0.287
Consumer	0.0628	0.243
Other products	0.0994	0.299
Industrial	0.0507	0.219
Biotechnology	0.0906	0.287
Computer HW	0.0270	0.162
Semiconductors	0.0663	0.249
Medical/Health	0.1000	0.300
VC experience	1.8359	0.781
LSE	56.8070	193.624
Venture's age	5.7053	3.196

Table 1.2 Correlations among the main variables

		1	2	3	4	5	6	7	8	9	10	11	12
1	Successful exit												
2	Extra-industry	0.01											
3	Intra-industry	0.00	0.68										
4	Interaction	0.01	0.70	0.81									
5	Concentration	-0.03	0.20	0.06	-0.02								
6	Proportion of ties	0.00	0.34	-0.02	0.08	0.42							
7	Co-investors	0.02	0.01	0.01	0.01	0.03	0.03						
8	Age at financing	-0.01	0.01	0.00	0.00	0.05	0.04	0.00					
9	VC/Venture=city	0.01	0.01	0.04	0.02	0.00	-0.03	-0.04	-0.08				
10	UK fund	-0.01	0.02	0.01	0.01	0.06	0.05	-0.11	0.04	0.25			
11	VC experience	0.05	0.00	-0.01	-0.01	0.07	0.02	0.11	0.07	-0.16	-0.12		
12	LSE	0.00	-0.05	0.03	-0.02	0.08	-0.20	-0.03	-0.03	0.02	-0.01	0.00	
13	Venture's age	0.09	0.00	-0.01	-0.03	0.03	0.07	0.10	0.58	-0.06	0.03	0.00	-0.15

Table 1.3 reports results of the logistic regression. At the first step, we entered the control variables. Not surprisingly, in hot market conditions (*LSE*) ventures have higher probabilities to reach a successful exit. Furthermore, in line with the literature, although not significant in this model, *VC experience* positively impacts the success of the firm. Moreover, even though older ventures have higher probability of exiting successfully, the earlier the firm receives its VC investment, the higher its likelihood of success. Finally, geographical proximity with the investor, in terms of city but not country, has a strong impact on the successful exit of the venture.

Table 1.3 Random effects panel logistic regression

Dependent variable: Successful exit					
Control Variables	**Model 1**	**Model 2**	**Model 3**	**Model 4**	**Model 5**
Co-investors	-0.03[†]	-0.03[†]	-0.03[†]	-0.03	-0.03
	(0.02)	(0.02)	(0.02)	(0.02)	(0.02)
Age at Financing	-0.02**	-0.02**	-0.02**	-0.02**	-0.02**
	(0.00)	(0.00)	(0.00)	(0.00)	(0.00)
VC/ Venture=City	0.27[†]	0.29*	0.30*	0.29[†]	0.29*
	(0.14)	(0.14)	(0.15)	(0.15)	(0.15)
UK Fund	-0.24[†]	-0.25[†]	-0.24[†]	-0.21	-0.21
	(0.13)	(0.13)	(0.13)	(0.13)	(0.13)
VC Experience	0.11	0.11	0.12	0.14[†]	0.14[†]
	(0.07)	(0.07)	(0.07)	(0.07)	(0.07)
LSE	0.00*	0.00*	0.00**	0.00**	0.00**
	(0.00)	(0.00)	(0.00)	(0.00)	(0.00)
Venture's Age	0.25**	0.25**	0.26**	0.26**	0.26**
	(0.03)	(0.03)	(0.03)	(0.03)	(0.03)
Network measures	**Model 1**	**Model 2**	**Model 3**	**Model 4**	**Model 5**
Intra-Industry[a]		-0.17*	-0.40**	-0.39**	-0.37**
		(0.08)	(0.12)	(0.12)	(0.12)
Extra-Industry[a]		0.19**	0.12[†]	0.22**	0.19*
		(0.06)	(0.06)	(0.07)	(0.08)
Interaction Intra*Extra			0.07**	0.05[†]	0.05*
			(0.02)	(0.02)	(0.02)
Concentration of ties[a]				-0.25**	
				(0.07)	

Continued

Table 1.3 Random effects panel logistic regression

Network Measures	Model 1	Model 2	Model 3	Model 4	Model 5
\multicolumn{6}{c}{Dependent variable: Successful exit}					
Proportion of Intra-industry ties					2.80** (0.77)
Proportion of Intra-industry ties^2					-3.28** (0.96)
Constant	-3.803** (0.58)	-3.752** (0.58)	-3.163** (0.40)	-4.01** (0.41)	-4.44** (0.49)
Industry dummies	YES	YES	YES	YES	YES
Fund stage dummies	YES	YES	YES	YES	YES
Wald chi-square	95.8**	102.71**	105.43**	105.88**	107.47**
Log likelihood	-1417.2	-1413.3	-1409.1	-1401.6	-1401.0

** $p<0.01$, * $p<0.05$, $^\dagger p<0.10$. [a] Represents measures centralized around the Z-score.

In the second step, we entered our main independent variables to test our hypotheses. H1 suggests that the venture's success will be positively (negatively) associated with *extra-industry (intra-industry)* ties. In model 2, we find support for this hypothesis since the *extra-industry* ties' coefficient is positive and highly significant ($p < .001$) and *intra-industry ties'* coefficient is negative and significant ($p < .05$).

In the third step, we test our H2a that posits that there is a positive interaction effect between ties. Put simply, the higher the amount of one type of tie, the higher the benefits received from the other ties, and vice versa. In model 3, we include the interaction effect between the two types of networks and we find that is positive and highly significant ($p < .001$). Therefore, we demonstrate that the two types of networks complement each other as hypothesized in H2a.

In the last steps (models 4 to 5), we test H2b that predicts that the optimal portfolio of ties is composed by both types of ties. In model 4, we insert the measure that represents the concentration of ties. If our hypothesis is supported, this variable has to be negative, showing that the higher the concentration of ties, the lower is the firm's likelihood of success. Hence, since the coefficient is negative and highly significant ($p <$ .001), we find support for H2b. Furthermore, in order to shed additional light on the optimal portfolio composition, in model 5 we introduce the proportion of *intra-industry* ties and its squared measures. In unreported analyses, we tested the impact of the proportion of *extra-industry* ties and the results are consistent. Since both squared measures are negative, we conclude that a diversified set of ties is preferable, and the optimum combination is centered around *extra-industry* connections.[15]

Looking at the overall fit of each of the models indicated by their log likelihoods and associated Wald chi-squares, it can be noted that the introduction of the amounts of ties in model 2 significantly improves the fit of the base model. Another significant improvement occurred in models 3 with the introduction of the interaction effect. Finally, there is a notable improvement in model 4 and 5 compared to model 2, with the introduction of the variables for concentration of ties, and the proportion of each type of ties. Figure 1.1 summarizes these main effects showing the impact of our independent variables, the combination of the two, and their proportion on the likelihood of success. In all the graphs, the *y*-axis represents the likelihood of having a successful exit.

The top graph in Figure 1.1 shows the impact of intra- and extra-industry *ties* on companies' performance. Clearly, the higher the amount of connections outside of the focal firm's industry, the better the performance. On the other hand, connections in the same industry hinder firm's performances. The graph in the left corner of Figure 1.1 illustrates that once a firm moves away from a balanced set of connections its performance will be affected. Similarly, as previously discussed (right corner graph), a balanced combination of ties is preferable over a concentrated distribution. It can be noted that once a firm has a portfolio with more than 40 percent of *intra-industry* ties, it will have lower chances of success. On the other hand, a firm that goes over a proportion of *extra-industry* ties of about 60 percent will reduce its likelihood of success. Hence, the best combination of intra- and extra-industry ties seems to be approximately 40/60 percent, respectively.

---

[15] Note that we cannot include in the same model both proportion of ties as they are symmetric.

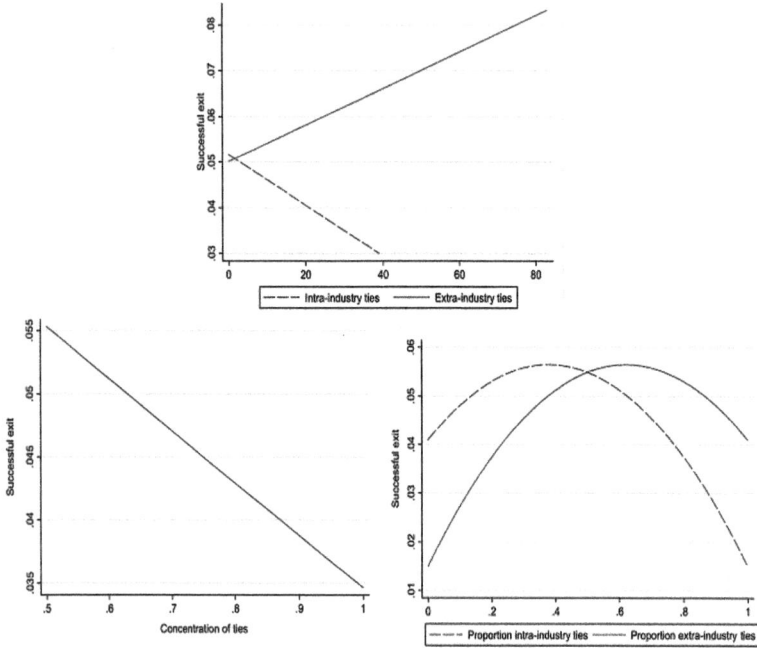

Figure 1.1 Main network effects

1.5.1 Robustness Tests

We conducted several robustness tests. First, we run different specifications of the model using panel regression (*xtreg*) and we obtained
similar results with the directions and significances of the main effects
remaining constant. In addition, we run a fixed-effect model without the
time-invariant measures, and the direction of the coefficients is consistent
but the significance is lower. Furthermore, we re-run the same type of
regression but instead of using a raw amount of ties we included more
elaborate measures such as *betweenness, eigenvector*, and *Bonacich power*
created from intra- and extra-industry matrices. In addition, we also
"weighted" the connections between firms by the geographical distance
between the two ventures; in all these tests, we had the same direction of
the coefficients although we found lower statistical significance for our
measures. Finally, in order to rule out the possibility that more successful
firms become more connected (a reverse causality argument), we lagged
our network measures by two years, and the results remain unchanged
and statistically significant.

1.6   Discussion and Conclusions

This study reveals that the configuration of intra- and extra-industry networks can explain both positive and negative performance of a firm. We provide empirical support to arguments by Podolny and Baron (1997) and Peng and Luo (2000) and demonstrate that not all ties and networks have the same impact on performance. Although the total amount of ties has a positive effect on performance, we demonstrate that different ties have different impacts. First, *extra-industry ties* give access to new information and knowledge (Christensen and Raynor 2003; Duysters 1996) and, in turn, increase company performance. This finding shows that in innovative and dynamic contexts firms gain more benefits from accessing novel knowledge which is likely to be found outside the industry of operations rather than from simply increasing the number of ties.

Second, young firms backed by VCs do not benefit directly from *intra-industry* ties. We argue that, in this context, the VC is a strong mediator of the resources that a venture gains in its industry, therefore mitigating the network benefits. However, as highlighted by Gargiulo and Benassi (2000) and Baden-Fuller et al. (2011), networks are costly to maintain and in our case it appears that these costs are not offset by the *intra-industry* network advantages. However, we also find that, once a venture manages to connect with an extensive amount of firms outside its industry, it is able to profit from the connections in its industry of operation as well. Put differently, although the *intra-industry* network taken independently has a negative impact, once a venture establishes a critical mass of *extra-industry* ties, it is able to benefit from its *intra-industry* ties. Figure 1.1 illustrates that the processes behind the impact of ties on shaping company performance are not straightforward, and there is an optimal combination of ties that involves both types of connections. We posit that, in order to thrive, a new firm needs to have a richer set of ties which provides access to different types of resources and opportunities.

1.7   Contributions

Research has only started to recognize and systematize the value of knowledge, technologies, and partners located in different industries (Enkel and

Gassmann 2010). Within this field of research, this study provides several contributions. First, we show empirically that the effects of intra- and extra-industry ties on firm performance are different but inextricably linked. Taken in isolation, *intra-industry* ties do not seem to offset the cost of managing them. However, once they are coupled with *extra-industry* ties, it looks like a firm manages to profit from both types of ties. Hence, we show that different ties mutually shape their contribution to firm performance. The fact that *intra-industry* centrality and *extra-industry* bridging ties have complementary effects on ventures' success provides initial empirical support for recent research arguing that internal and external social capital may have interactive effects (Mehra et al. 2006; Oh et al. 2004; Stam and Elfring 2008). Supporting the notion that social capital has contingent value (Ahuja 2000), in particular in relation to the nature and content of the ties, this study shows that different network configurations shape the effect of networks and that different types of networks affect each other's value. The results highlight the need to examine not only the interactions among different forms of social capital, but also the contingencies that determine the optimal balance of ties.

Second, this study also advances literature pointing to the "dark side" of social capital (Baden-Fuller et al. 2011; Gargiulo and Benassi 2000). The results emphasize that by simultaneously examining different types of networks, we offer a better understanding of the conditions under which network centrality is detrimental to performance. Previous research has shown that firms can become over embedded in cohesive networks of strong ties (Uzzi 1997). Accordingly, as suggested by Stam and Elfring (2008), over-embeddedness can also be viewed as an imbalance between internal and external social capital. This idea suggests that considering a firm's embeddedness only in one network may generate misleading results due to overlooking other types of networks. Borrowing from Stam and Elfring (2008), we examined the optimal configuration of a firm's ties across multiple networks and showed that a balanced set of ties, with a stronger presence of *extra-industry* ties, is needed to succeed in an entrepreneurial setting.

Third, we contribute to the long-standing debate between closure (Coleman 1988) and structural holes (Burt 2001). In line with Burt's argument, we show that a firm that has access to different industry segments gains new knowledge and with this background can profit from its *intra-industry* network centrality. However, we show that structural holes are important not only because they connect unconnected firms, but also because they connect unconnected industry segments. Future research may look at the differences between structural holes that connect companies in the same or unrelated industries.

Lastly, although the importance of networks in the VC world has been demonstrated, we believe that this is the first attempt to assess the value of the connections that a firm has access to through a portfolio of VC-backed companies. Consistent with the view that VCs provide more than capital, we find that investors add value to their investee companies, providing a fruitful environment for collaboration among their companies. This finding is supported by both archival data and by interviews with VC managers. In practice, VCs promote a vibrant environment organizing recurring summits where all the portfolio companies are invited, by linking these companies directly, and by creating databases that connect the CEOs and CTOs of their companies for a joint problem-solving. We extend the VC literature that advocates the value adding activities provided by the VCs (for an extensive review, see Manigart and Wright 2014; Karlson et al. 2017). Contributing to this research, we show that VCs provide access to a potentially valuable network composed by their portfolio companies. However, not all companies benefit from all the connections but rather it is important to establish the right links within this network.

1.8   Limitations and Directions for Future Research

Our results have several implications for the current debate on the relationship between networks and success. However, we would like to acknowledge some limitations and recommend caution when extracting conclusions, and suggest the importance of future research on the topic. The main limitation of this research is that it cannot demonstrate whether an alliance has been really established or that a VC effectively initiated a collaboration between portfolio companies. However, according to Powell et al. (1996) exploratory study, the official partnerships are just a small portion of the entirety. Similarly, Hite (2005) argues that embedded ties are generally governed through informal mechanisms of relational governance such as trust and relational contracting rather than through more formal mechanisms of market governance such as contracts (Granovetter 1985; Uzzi 1996, 1997; Williamson 1979; Zaheer and Venkataraman 1995). Furthermore, as it has been mentioned by VCs and entrepreneurs that we have interviewed, only a small portion of these collaborations is contractualized and that the VC is "a small world governed by trust." Therefore, if we would consider only the joint ventures publicly communicated, we would lose all the other indirect information and resource exchanges that are fundamental to the success of the new firms. However, further research could include more fine-grained networks' measures, for instance, combining official alliances with measures of informal collaborations. In addition considering the highly significant personal networks of VCs and entrepreneurs, both formal and informal, would offer interesting insights.

Furthermore, our network measure is based on horizontal firm differentiation (e.g., different industries); hence we do not control for ties spanning across vertical sectors. For example, would the *intra-industry* ties effect be the same if the two companies operate in different points of the value chain? Or maybe this type of ties provides the same, if not higher, benefits than *extra-industry* ties? A useful extension of this research would examine both intra- and extra-industry ties, as well as vertical versus horizontal ties.

Furthermore, a very interesting avenue for future research is represented by the different degree of network effectiveness contingent on the life cycle of the firm. In their conceptual study, Hite and Hesterly (2001) postulate that the networks of emerging firms evolve in response to the changing resource's needs and acquisition challenges of the firm as it moves through the life cycle stages of emergence and early growth. This dynamic network evolution is the process by which firms strategically adapt and align their networks to gain the resources they need to ensure successful emergence and early growth (e.g., Golden and Dollinger 1993; Ostgaard and Birley 1994). Therefore, testing the contingent effect of resource availability accessible through intra- and extra-industry networks and life cycle of the firm is a promising extension of this study. In fact, it can be hypothesized, borrowing from the resource-based notion, that firms cooperate in order to gain access to critical resources and considering that older firms *pari passu* have higher resources, they will gain less benefit from wider networks.

Moreover, we looked at the success of the venture in reaching a positive exit. It would be interesting to see what is the impact of different types of ties on innovation, and as well how innovation shapes the network configuration of a firm. For example, are new ventures more inclined to partner with an innovative firm in their industry rather than with an outsider?

Finally, we considered only one market, the UK, in one particular context, the VC industry. This leads us to concerns about generalizability of our findings. It would be interesting to understand the impact of different networks of portfolio companies in other markets, potentially taking into consideration institutional factors. This network can be centered in other countries or take into account cross-country relationships. Therefore testing whether institutional factors such as Intellectual Property (IP) protection or cultural factors have an impact on this knowledge sharing is an interesting question that we leave unanswered.

1.9   Practical Implications

Possible limitations notwithstanding, the present research offers several practical implications. The findings reveal that entrepreneurs can enhance the performance of their ventures by simultaneously increasing the amount of *extra-industry* ties and at the same time connecting with ventures in their industry. Yet, entrepreneurs should be aware that a strong balance in favor of *intra-industry* ties may constrain performances when an *intra-industry* centrality is not accommodated by sufficient *extra-industry* bridging ties. Considering this potential trade-off between building different social capital conduits, an important challenge for entrepreneurs concerns balancing their efforts at strengthening their intra- and extra-industry networks simultaneously and strategically. Entrepreneurs are encouraged to support initiatives that may foster the development of *intra-industry* ties, but at the same time, the findings suggest that such networking activities may be costly to manage and do not provide the expected benefits if are not complemented by initiatives that support the creation of *extra-industry* ties. Furthermore, in addition to considering the different value adding activities and resources offered by a VC, when approaching investors the entrepreneurs should look at what companies they can gain access to through their investors to be; companies may be better off by selecting VCs that focus on diverse industries so that they obtain financing from highly specialized VCs but at the same time accessing opportunities with portfolio companies in different industries. Symmetrically, VCs should invest in new ventures not only for their potential, but also for their network that may in turn benefit their portfolio companies.

CHAPTER 2

The Impact of Investment Networks on Venture Capital Firm Performance

A Contingency Framework

Venture capital (VC) syndicates involve repeated transactions among partners and, therefore, they possess network-like characteristics. Although networks provide access to important externalities, extant literature has not studied the effects of the focal firm's resource needs on performance benefits arising from different network structures. We investigate the impact of the VC firm's maturity and status as proxies for firm-level resources on the relationship between network cohesion and VC performance. Analyzing a dataset of the UK VC investments (1998–2012), we find that mature/high-status VCs benefit less from network cohesion, and they are better off when joining networks rich in structural holes. We also show that maturity and status act in concert by simultaneously determining performance effects of the specific network structure.

2.1   Introduction

Syndicates are a common practice in various financial markets including VC investments (Manigart et al. 2006) and bank lending (Song 2004). Syndicates are formed when a group of financiers makes a joint decision to provide finance under conditions of uncertainty, and payoffs are subsequently shared among them (Lerner 1994). In the entrepreneurial finance context, prior studies indicate that the majority of VC investments are syndicated (Jääskeläinen et al. 2006; Jääskeläinen 2012), and this practice "creates a network of relations within the VC community" (Sorenson and Stuart 2001: 1559). VC syndicates often involve repeated transactions among partners that lead to the formation of network-based relationships (Bygrave 1988; Hochberg et al. 2007, 2010; Hsu 2004), and VCs "are bound by their current and past investments into webs of relationships with other VCs" (Hochberg et al. 2007: 251). However, there is very little research on structural characteristics of VC syndication networks and how they affect performance of individual syndicate members.

When selecting co-investment partners, a VC firm has to make a decision on whether it wants to be a member of a cohesive network or networks rich in structural holes. When a VC firm syndicates with interconnected partners (VC firms that consistently co-invest with each other), it joins a cohesive investor network. Alternatively, it may syndicate with VCs that do not invest with each other but form investment ties with new VCs, and, therefore, it joins an investor network rich in structural holes (Echols and Tsai 2005; Podolny 2001). The debate related to the cost–benefit trade-offs associated with membership of cohesive versus structural holes networks has become one of the most prominent conversations in the network literature, fueled by a considerable ambiguity in empirical findings (Echols and Tsai 2005; Shipilov and Li 2008). For example, previous studies associate a cohesive network with enhanced reputation and trust considerations that govern transactions within a group of firms. By promoting mutual monitoring and enforcement of norms that reduce partner opportunism, it enhances an environment of trust and facilitates the flow of resources within the network (Coleman 1988). Hence, cohesive networks should be beneficial for their individual members. However, Burt (1992) demonstrates that social constraints arising within a cohesive network limit the actor's flexibility and the scope of exchange in non-redundant resources. Burt (1992) emphasizes opportunities provided within a network rich in structural holes that supplies non-redundant resources and allows for brokerage opportunities that network members may enjoy. From this perspective, networks with structural holes should be more beneficial for their members. Although network studies have emphasized the relevance of network structural characteristics (cohesion vs. structural holes) for organizations, there is a dearth of research exploring the impact of networks associated with investment syndication on the performance of an individual syndicate member. Our study aims to shed light on the effect of the structural characteristics of VC syndication networks on the performance of individual VCs.

Previous research within the broader network literature has mainly focused on various externalities associated with cohesive or structural holes networks, such as formation of trust, information exchange, and the flow of non-redundant resources among the network members. As indicated above, these studies are inconclusive in determining which type of network structure is more beneficial for a member firm (Kilduff and Brass 2010). "One reason for a lack of consistent findings is that firms differ greatly [...], and such differences have not been considered yet" (Echols and Tsai 2005: 233). In particular, previous network research has focused predominantly on the network's ability to supply relevant resources to the focal firm (e.g., Dahlander and Frederiksen 2011; Gargiulo and Benassi 2000; Gulati 1999; Hite and Hesterly 2001; Phelps 2010; Stuart et al. 1999), and it overlooked differences between firms in terms of their idiosyncratic resource needs (Oh et al. 2004). In other words, extant research has extensively studied the supply side of network resources from the focal firm's perspective, and less attention has been paid to the demand side which may depend on a number of firm-level resource contingencies. As Bae and Gargiulo (2004: 857) argue, "a joint consideration of actors' resources and of the social structure in which those resources are exchanged will lead to better understanding of the economic consequences of social relations," and this is a focal theoretical lens we apply in our study of VC networks.

To understand whether VC firms are better off entering a cohesive syndication network as opposed to placing themselves in a structural holes position, we build on a contingency approach to exploring the effects of network characteristics (Ahuja 2000). We argue that the benefits associated with a particular network structure are contingent upon complementarity and fit between resources accessible through the network and resources already controlled by the firm. More specifically, in the context of VC industry, we focus on VC maturity and status as important firm-level factors that may help to unambiguously determine the balance between costs and benefits of different network structural characteristics from the focal firm's perspective that so far has eluded network researchers. The maturity of a VC is an indication of its strong resource position vis-a-vis younger, recently formed funds (Gompers 1996; Petty and Gruber 2011). Mature VC firms have better access to financial resources provided by limited partners, more experience with selecting better investment targets, and higher ability to develop and sell successful ventures compared to their newly established peers (Gompers et al. 2008). The VC firm's status is another important firm-level factor that underpins a favorable exchange position with regard to other firms (Podolny 1993, 2001, 2005). High-status VCs are more visible within VC community, and they are more likely to be invited to join syndicates organized by other VCs. By jointly considering these firm-level characteristics and network structure, we explore the following research question: *What are the effects of the focal VC firm's maturity and status on the relationship between network cohesion (versus structural holes) and the VC's performance?*

This research makes a number of contributions to both network and entrepreneurial finance literatures. First, we develop a framework within which we not only consider the network's supply of resources, but also the focal firm's demand for those resources within both cohesive networks and networks rich in structural holes. We argue that the focal firm's resource endowment shapes the performance benefits arising from particular network structures. Considering both the firm's and the network's resources is an important contribution to the network literature that currently lacks a resource-based view of social capital (Oh et al. 2004). Second, within this general resource-based framework, we identify two specific and important contingencies that moderate the "network cohesion–firm performance" relationship: the firm's maturity and its status. Therefore, we contribute to more recent literature that aims to develop a more contextualized, contingency perspective on costs and benefits associated with different network structures (Battilana and Casciaro 2012; Baum et al. 2012; Shipilov 2006, 2009; Tortoriello et al. 2012; Venkatraman et al. 2008). More specifically, by introducing the firm's maturity and status as novel contingency factors we shed additional light on the long-standing debate between the benefits of cohesion (Coleman 1988) and structural holes (Burt 1992) which, despite its strategic relevance, still remains an unresolved issue in the network literature (Kilduff and Brass 2010). Third, we advance the entrepreneurial finance literature by applying our theoretical framework to the VC industry. In particular, we show that VC syndicates are formal investment networks that can have different structural characteristics that, in turn, offer significantly different performance advantages to VCs with different levels of maturity and status.

We empirically test our hypotheses using an extensive dataset of firm-level investments by VCs in the UK. We focus on VC exits as a performance proxy since it represents a key strategic outcome of the investment syndication process (Abell and Nisar 2007). The number of portfolio company exits through an IPO or trade sale is an important measure of performance of VC firms (Matusik and Fitza 2012). We find that younger, low-status VC firms have better performance when they join a cohesive network with other VC investors, while a network with structural holes is more beneficial for mature and high-status firms. Finally, using a three-way interaction model, we show that the effects of firm's maturity and status strengthen each other. Therefore, they have jointly determined effects in terms of shaping the cost–benefit trade-offs associated with cohesiveness and/or structural holes within syndication networks.

2.2   Theory and Hypotheses

Financial syndicates received considerable attention in finance (e.g., Hochberg et al. 2007, 2010), strategy (e.g., Echols and Tsai 2005), sociology (Ma et al. 2013), and entrepreneurship (e.g., Lockett et al. 2006) literatures. The VC financing represents a "networked industry" (Bygrave 1988; Echols and Tsai 2005), and VC syndicates are an important mechanism to access network resources (Gargiulo and Benassi 2000; Hite and Hesterly 2001; Stuart et al. 1999) and diversify risks (Manigart et al. 2006). Through syndicates VCs are able to improve their selection process and value adding capabilities, as well as gain wider access to different entrepreneurial ventures in need of external financing (Bygrave 1988; Hochberg et al. 2007; Lerner 1994).

Yet, although syndication and investment networks have the potential to improve performance of individual VCs by promoting mutual support and trust, they are also associated with significant agency risks, coordination costs, and exchange of redundant information (Filatotchev et al. 2006; Steier and Greenwood 1995; Wright and Lockett 2003). This cost–benefit trade-off associated with network membership becomes particularly explicit in the analysis of one important characteristic of the VC syndication network structure, namely network cohesion as opposed to structural holes.

More recently the literature posited that both cohesion and structural holes can be advantageous under different contextual conditions (Burt 2001; Kilduff and Brass 2010; Reagans and McEvily 2003). Researchers have empirically tested a number of contingencies that fall into three broad categories. First, scholars focused on the network context. For example, the performance benefits of structural holes decrease with ties' age (Baum et al. 2012) and increase with ties' strength (Tortoriello et al. 2012), diversity (Phelps 2010), and ties' "imprinting effect" (McEvily et al. 2012). Second, research considered changes in the firm's environment as important moderators of the network structure–performance relationship. For example, some researchers argue that network cohesion may not be beneficial in a changing economic environment or a fast-pace industry because managers in cohesive networks are less likely to adapt (Battilana and Casciaro 2012; Gargiulo and Benassi 2000; Rowley et al. 2000). Third, scholars focused on the moderating effects of business strategy. The firm's diversification as opposed to specialization (Shipilov 2006; Venkatraman et al., 2008), capacity to absorb heterogeneous information, bargaining power, and ability to protect against partner noncooperation (Shipilov 2009) all increase the benefits of a network with structural holes. We build on this literature by arguing that the focal firm's resources represent additional, and relatively less explored, firm-level contingency factors that shape the relationship between network structure and performance.

Although it has been recognized that networks provide access to resources (Amit et al. 1990; Ensley et al. 2002; Hopp 2009), extant network research has overlooked the demand side of network resources, which, in turn, depends on the existing resource endowment of an individual network member. Even within the same network, resource requirements vary between member organizations and for the same firm in different moments of its development. Therefore, we argue that different network structures may offer different performance advantages to the focal firm depending on its resource-related characteristics. In particular, we propose two factors that account for resource differences across VC firms that, in turn, impact the effect of each network structure on firm performance: (a) the VC firm's maturity that reflects evolution of internal resources such as investment experience, access to capital, and market knowledge, and (b) the firm's status that determines potential external resource advantages associated with the perception that other firms have of the focal VC. Maturity and status capture variation of resource needs not only across firms, but also with regard to the same firm in different periods of its life. In the subsequent sections, we discuss how these two important contingencies may affect the network structure–performance relationship, and offer a number of testable hypotheses.

2.2.1 Network Cohesion and the VC Firm's Maturity

Young firms differ considerably from mature firms in their resource challenges and endowments and, everything else being equal, they have fewer resources than mature firms (Hite and Hesterley 2001). This logic is particularly relevant in the context of the VC industry. VCs need time and effort to build up their resources such as an established management structure or relevant industry and investment experience (Bygrave 1987; Bygrave and Timmons 1992). As VCs mature they gain "investment experience in a particular sector and are more likely to acquire the expertise needed to help start-ups in their portfolio" (Hsu 2004: 1809).

This resource difference is evident when comparing first and follow-on funds. First-time funds have, as a rule, lower financial resources than follow-on funds (Petty and Gruber 2011: 182). More importantly, younger funds have fewer intangible, knowledge-related resources. As Petty and Gruber (2011: 183) explained, VCs "gain experience in deal evaluation and portfolio management within Fund I, which in turn allow the firms to spend additional time on preinvestment activities in Fund II and also help the VC to avoid the costs associated with an investment in an unsuccessful venture." Therefore, there is a considerable difference between young and mature VC firms in terms of making successful investments. In partic-ular, mature firms, due to their market and investment experience, are in a better position to select the most promising start-ups and add value to their portfolio companies leading them to a successful exit.

Young firms can alleviate their internal resource constraints by participating in a cohesive network. A cohesive network is based on a relational exchange, rather than market dynamics (Zaheer and Venkataraman 1995) and, therefore, it is more likely to provide resources needed by a young firm at a relatively low cost (Hite and Hesterly 2001; Starr and Macmillan 1990) and without the need for a short-run reciprocation (Baum 1996). Although a newly established VC has fewer opportunities to add value to a start-up due to its limited market and investment knowledge, by co-investing with a close circle of partners, it will be able to rely on their expertise to add value to the investee company. Furthermore, during the investment process, a young VC is at higher risk of self-serving behavior by other syndicate members which Filatotchev et al. (2006) describe as "principal-principal" agency risks. These potential conflicts of interests within a syndicate may expose a young VC firm to exploitation by more established peers. Therefore, young firms will be better off in a cohesive network where social norms would mitigate dangers of self-serving partner behavior (Coleman 1988; Reagans and McEvily 2003).

Although the socially embedded mechanism of mutual support typical of a cohesive network is important during the early phase of the VC firm's development, it may limit firm flexibility and opportunities during the maturity stage. A young VC firm controls a scarce amount of resources, and the social dynamics embedded in a cohesive network will prevent the firm from failing and support its growth. However, a mature firm requires less protection from the network. Rather, it needs opportunities to grow further and sustain its performance, and structural holes provide better access to new business opportunities (Shipilov and Li 2008). In addition, although social constraints derived from a cohesive network offer protection, they may limit flexibility and partner diversity necessary to thrive in the dynamic VC industry in the long term.

These arguments suggest that, once the VC firm matures and gains a competitive position, a limited flexibility may expose it to future risks if the competitive landscape changes and the firm is not fast enough to adapt to the new environment (Hannan and Freeman 1984). As Kogut et al. (2007) show, although co-investing with the same partners over time provides advantages, this may compromise the firm's ability to enter into new, more lucrative markets even when it has enough financial resources and deal-making expertise to do so. Considering that the VC industry is a dynamic and cyclical environment that changes fast and recurrently (Gompers et al. 2008), flexibility is a key strategic component.

For example, "green economy" firms and industries have received significant investments at the turn of the 21st century, but recently they faced a decline in VC funding, which has shifted toward social network companies such as Facebook, Twitter, LinkedIn, and Zynga. Therefore, if at the beginning of the 2000s a VC firm was partnering consistently with the same cohesive group of VCs specializing in the green economy, it would more likely have missed a shift in investment landscape toward the social network sector. Bearing in mind that both relationships and resources, within cohesive networks, are likely to be high in redundancy and low in diversity (Burt 1992), any attempts by the focal VC to learn about the social network industry would be constrained by its green economy-focused VC network. As a result, membership in a cohesive network may limit the VC firm's knowledge acquisition and recognition of development opportunities (Shipilov and Li 2008) that would have enhanced growth in the long term (Baum et al. 2000; McEvily and Zaheer 1999). Therefore, once a mature VC firm builds up internal resources, a structural holes position will help it to access nonredundant resources, to be aware of market shifts and to achieve better the overall performance.

These arguments suggest that the VC firm's maturity may be an important firm-level contingency factor that affects the relationship between network structure and VC performance. Hence, we suggest the following hypothesis:

H1: The relationship between VC network cohesion and individual VC firm performance is contingent on the firm's maturity. Specifically, for younger (more mature) VC firms, membership of a cohesive (structural holes) network improves performance.

2.2.2 Network Cohesion and the VC Firm's Status

Our arguments above suggest that the VC firm's maturity, as a proxy of its ability to identify and grow successful ventures, may determine the inter-relationship between network structural characteristics and performance. In this section, we focus on how the firm can take advantage of its ability to marshal external resources associated with its status (Podolny 1993, 2001, 2005). High-status VC firms are desirable partners (Dimov and Milanov 2010; Podolny 1994) and are therefore more likely to attract external investors (e.g., limited partners), syndication partners as well as prospective investee companies (Benjamin and Podolny 1999; Fombrun and Shanley 1990; Hopp 2009; Ozmel et al. 2013; Podolny 1993, 1994, 2001; Pollock et al. 2010; Stuart et al. 1999). In addition, status facilitates access to external expertise and offers a superior ability to leverage information and reach out to socially distant potential partners (Dimov and Milanov 2010). High-status VC firms are more likely to build relationships with prestigious investment banks/underwriters (Gulati and Higgins 2003), and, as a result, have higher chances to achieve a successful exit from their portfolio companies that enhances their performance (Hochberg et al. 2007). On the other hand, a low-status firm is an unattractive partner and therefore will be in a disadvantageous position in terms of partnering with top peers or being invited to join the most promising syndicates.

However, a low-status firm can mitigate these disadvantages and enhance its access to external resources by being part of a cohesive VC network. In this context, social capital can act as a substitute for the lack of status, and even a low-status VC may be able to have access to a higher number and higher quality investment opportunities. The network cohesion offers a social mechanism that facilitates a spill-over of benefits from high-status VCs to their lower-status peers, such as links with prestigious underwriters, visibility benefits, and higher legitimacy among market audiences (Suchman 1995).

Following the same logic, a high-status VC firm will not need a cohesive network to partner with equally high-status VCs. Rather, in a cohesive network, high-status firms may suffer network pressures to collaborate with firms of lower status. On the other hand, a structural-hole position offers high-status VCs opportunities associated with diversity and brokerage potential. High-status VCs are able to choose their partners and, therefore, have the possibility to be embedded in different networks that offer diverse investment opportunities. In addition, a network rich in structural holes allows a high-status firm to broker relationship and profit from those exchanges. In this type of network, a high-status VC is well positioned to act as a broker as the disconnected actors would trust more a high-status intermediary (Podolny 2001). For example, the lead VC in a syndicate acts as a broker inviting other firms to participate in the deal and sets the valuation and investment conditions. Hence the status of the focal VC is an important factor that the other partners consider to evaluate the firm's reliability and consequently accept the investment conditions.

In sum, status is an important firm attribute that provides access to external resources. In particular, high-status VCs have higher chances to be invited in top syndicates and have the opportunity to be in a brokerage position. Therefore, high-status VCs can benefit from a structural-holes network that will offer non-redundant investment opportunities and brokerage potential. On the other hand, low-status VCs need a cohesive network to be invited to promising co-investment opportunities, even if they lack the status of a desirable partner. These arguments lead us to our second hypothesis:

H2: The relationship between VC network cohesion and individual VC firm performance is contingent on the firm's status. Specifically, for lower (higher) status VC firms, membership in a cohesive (structural holes) network improves performance.

2.2.3 Maturity, Status, and Network Structure: A Three-way Interaction

Our previous arguments suggest that the VC firm's status and maturity are important contingency factors that affect the impact of network structural characteristics on the focal firm's performance. We extend these arguments further and suggest that these effects of firm's maturity and status are not orthogonal but mutually reinforcing. A young firm may have either high or low status. Similarly, although a firm may have gained a high-status position as it evolved along its life-cycle, this is not always the case as some mature firms may have a low status. Therefore, our final premise is that the impact of network characteristics on the VC firm's performance will depend on a constellation of the two contingency factors, in line with more recent configurational research (see Bell et al. 2014, for a review).

We argue above that mature firms have higher capabilities that improve their selection process as well as their value adding activities. As a consequence, mature firms have higher potential to lead their start-ups to a successful exit. Furthermore, we suggest that mature firms are better off in a structural holes network since they can identify better and more diverse investment opportunities to utilize their superior capabilities. However, although maturity is an important condition, it is not sufficient to be invited to co-invest with top players in the best deals and act as a broker in a structural holes network. We show that having high status is another critical factor for the VC firm to be positively perceived by external parties and, therefore, to be invited to participate in the best syndicates, as well as to be considered a reliable broker. These arguments jointly suggest that there may be a three-way interaction effect on the VC firm's performance of maturity, status, and network characteristics. Mature VCs have better capabilities and resources to help (advise) the venture, but these capabilities are most useful within networks with structural holes. Status offers the focal VC more opportunities to increase its deal flow by being approached by promising ventures or invited in VC syndicates. Status also offers better chances to exit via attracting prestigious investment banks and the public market investors. Again, when the focal VC firm is mature and has high status, a structural holes network will maximize the firm's performance.

On the other hand, a low-status and young VC firm is in a position where a cohesive network is the best network to be embedded in. In this type of network, the mechanisms of social cohesion may help the focal VC not only to identify and grow a venture toward a successful exit, but also provide important network externalities associated with an improved deal flow and important external connections, including investment banks.

This reasoning leads us to the following hypothesis suggesting a three-way interaction between maturity, status, and network structure:

H3: The relationship between VC network cohesion and individual VC firm performance is contingent on the interaction of firm's maturity and status. Specifically, for younger (more mature) VC firms with lower (higher) levels of status, membership in a cohesive (structural holes) network improves performance.

2.3   Methods

2.3.1 Data

The empirical context of this study is the VC industry in the UK. Several factors make this industry a useful research setting. In the VC industry, networks are very important (Manigart and Wright 2014), and it has been used as a research laboratory to conduct numerous network studies (e.g., Abell and Nisar 2007; Hochberg et al. 2007, 2010; Podolny 2001; Sorenson and Stuart 2001). We chose to focus on the UK VC market because, although being the most important VC market in Europe (EVCA, report on European VC activity 2012) and the third most attractive worldwide (Groh et al. 2013), it has received considerably less attention than the U.S. VC market (Bellavitis et al. 2014). The UK VC industry has financed some of the best new ventures around the world such as Last.fm, LoveFilm (Amazon), Mendeley, SoundCloud, SkyScanner, and many others.

Our unit of analysis is the VC firm, but we also collected data on the portfolio companies as venture exit from the VC portfolio is our proxy of VC performance. The primary source for investment data was the Thomson One Banker (previously Venture Expert) database that comprehensively reports VC investments worldwide. Individual VC firms have been selected based on the following criteria: (a) location, (b) stage and type, and (c) investment date. First, we included VC firms that invested in the UK firms to avoid sample variations with regard to macro-institutional factors (e.g., regulation, cultural dimensions) that can bias our findings. Second, we selected VC firms that focused on start-ups and excluded buy-outs, public-to-private transactions, and private equity deals outside new venture context. We selected only VCs that invested in ventures that have been in existence for eight years or less (Zahra 1996), including

VC investments from seed to later stages. Finally, we included VCs that invested in ventures that received their first round of funding between 1998 and 2008. Our records track the investment outcomes until September 2012 because VC portfolio companies require a few years to develop a venture and exit (Hochberg et al. 2007). The final dataset contains 1,235 VC-backed companies, including 1,954 deals made by 503 VC firms. In total, we have 351 VC exits through IPOs and trade sales, approximately 29 percent of the total number of portfolio companies. These figures are in line with those reported by the British Venture Capital Association for the available years within our period (2007–2012).

Building up on previous literature, we created a longitudinal dataset of co-investment networks among VC firms. In our setting, we coded two VCs co-investing in the same portfolio company as having a tie. By matching VC firms investing together in each year, we were able to create yearly adjacency matrices. Networks are not static. Relationships may change, and entry and exit from a network may change each VC networks (Hochberg et al. 2007). We constructed our adjacency matrices using a 5-year moving window. For example, if VC A and VC B invest together in 2002 we considered them to be connected for five years (from 2002 to 2006). This method is in line with previous VC and network studies (e.g., Gulati and Gargiulo 1999; Gulati et al. 2012; Ma et al. 2013). For example, Sorenson and Stuart (2001: 1568) noted that "if two firms have not co-invested within a five-year period, it seems unlikely that their members remain close confidants." We also collected yearly portfolio company exit data from Zephyr and MergerMarket databases. The final dataset has a total of 5,015 company-year observations.

2.3.2 Measures

In order to have a better understanding of our measures in the VC industry, we consulted seven experts: a partner of a consultancy firms specialized in VC fund raising, a legal counsel of a VC firm, three VC managers, and two CEOs of VC-backed firms, each employed by a different organization. We interviewed each of them to understand if the way we measured internal and external resources were robust in our context. All experts approved our choice and confirmed the face validity of our measures.

Performance

Previous studies indicate that the ultimate goal of VC firms is to exit their portfolio companies through either a trade sale or IPO. The amount of exits is a clear and objective way to assess performance of the VCs (Cumming 2007), and IPOs and trade sales are widely regarded as the best exit outcomes for VCs (Abell and Nisar 2007; Cumming et al. 2006; Cumming and MacIntosh 2003; Gompers and Lerner 1999; Manigart and Wright 2014). Alternative measures of success such as accounting ones may be misleading in this industry and are seldom available; both the portfolio companies and the VCs are private companies that rarely disclose their financial results (Bellavitis et al. 2014; Nahata 2008). Therefore, in order to test our hypotheses, we used the number of exits (both trade sales and IPOs) in a given year as a proxy of VC performance.

Network Cohesion

This variable estimates how cohesive a VC network is. We used the network constraint measure suggested by Burt (1992: 55) implemented in UciNet 6 (Borgatti et al. 2002):

$$C_{ij} = \left(P_{ij} + \sum_{Qxixj} P_{iq} P_{qj} \right)^2$$

In the above formula, the focal actor i has two contacts q and j, and it estimates how redundant and cohesive is the relationship i–j. P_{ij} reflects the interaction between i and j, while P_{qj} defines whether q and j are related. Therefore if the three VCs are all related, it is difficult to develop a structural hole, and the network is cohesive. The sum of the cohesiveness of all VC relationships defines the overall cohesion. This is a continuous variable with higher values reflecting cohesive networks and lower values indicating that the network is disperse and rich in structural holes.

Maturity

In order to determine the VC firm's maturity, we built upon Gompers (1996) that defined young VC firms as being in existence for six years or less. Our interviews with the industry participants confirmed that for the first five to six years a VC invests its first fund, and it is considered "early stage" or "a new player." After six years of investing, the VC firm focuses on harvesting its first fund (which on average takes another six years) as well as on raising and investing a second fund. In line with Gompers (1996), we did not use a continuous measure of age since the development of a VC fund is not linear. VC firms follow a clear pattern in which during the first years they invest their funds, then they start harvesting their investments and subsequently (based on their exit results) start raising follow-on funds. Usually these periods last approximately 5/6 years as the funds have a life span of 10/12 years (Hochberg et al. 2007). Therefore, using time interval proxies is more robust in terms of differentiating between different levels of maturity of VC firms (Gompers 1996). Yet, our interviews indicated that a binary measure with a six-year cut-off point used in most of previous studies may be over-simplistic, and that we need one more level of maturity. A general partner of a UK-based VC suggested: "you need an additional threshold since theoretically at this time [about 12 years] a fund manager will be on Fund III and will have at least one, possibly two other funds active." Therefore, we construct a three-stage maturity measure in which the first stage includes VC younger than 6 years (early stage firms), the second stage includes VC between 6 and 12 years old (maturing, mid-life firms), and the third stage includes VCs older than 12 years (mature firms). To test the sensitivity of our results to the chosen cut-off points, we tested different thresholds for the variable including the binary 6-year measure used by Gompers (1996) and obtained similar results (see section Robustness Tests for details).

Status

Following prior studies (Hallen 2008; Jensen 2003; Ma et al. 2013; Podolny 1993, 2001; Ozmel et al. 2013; Rider 2009), we operationalized a firm's status as its Bonacich (1987) centrality in the VC co-investment network using UciNet 6 (Borgatti et al. 2002). In particular, we adopt the procedure implemented by Ma et al. (2013). Each firm's Bonacich centrality was computed as follows:

$$C_{ij}(\alpha,\beta) = \sum A_{ij}(\alpha + \beta c_j)$$

where, α is a scaling factor that normalizes the measure in a given year, β is a weighting factor. Borrowing from Ma et al. (2013), to obtain the status score, we set β equal to zero (i.e., a VC firm's status is determined by how many partners with which it is directly affiliated). This β is also practically appropriate in the VC community (Ma et al. 2013).

Although both cohesion and status proxies are network measures, the two are clearly distinct. As Podolny (2001: 44) explains, there is an important trade-off between the formation of ties that will add structural holes and the formation of ties that will increase the focal firm's status. The measure of status considers how well *connected* a firm is, while the measure of cohesion (structural holes) measures how *interconnected* (disconnected) the connections of the focal VC are.

Control Variables

In order to rule out alternative explanations and avoid spurious correlations, we included three types of controls related to the VC firm, the portfolio company, and environmental conditions. In relation to the focal VC firm, we controlled for the average number of *Co-investors* for each VC over its life. Previous findings suggest that syndicated deals outperform solo investments (Lockett et al. 2006). We controlled for *VC experience* using the number of investments (a logarithm of the amount of companies invested in) and funds managed (a number of *Funds Under Management*). We expect both measures of experience to be positively associated with successful exits. We use two dummies (*U.S. fund* and *Other Non-UK Location fund*) for geographical differences (Sorenson and Stuart 2001). Expectations are that local VCs outperform foreign players. *Investment Diversification* (Matusik and Fitza 2012; Phalippou and Gottschalg 2009) is approximated by the Herfindahl index based on the six industries reported by the Venture Expert. Fulghieri and Sevilir (2009) suggest that investment focus is beneficial to VC performance, hence non-diversified VCs might outperform diversified investors. We also include a dummy equal to 1 when the VC is independent (*P.E. Investors Dummy*) as opposed to corporate or bank affiliated. Independent

VCs may have higher pressures to exit compared to captive ones. In addition, we control for the average portfolio company age at the first round of VC (*Venture Age at Financing*). If a start-up is older at the time of the VC investment, may be more developed and more likely to exit. Finally, we control for public markets conditions. We measure annual net new listings on the London Stock Exchange, *LSE* (Ozmel et al. 2013) and market *Competition* (yearly amount of VC investments). During boom periods (more listings and VC investment), the markets are more interested in VC-backed start-ups (Gompers et al. 2008) and therefore we may observe more exits.

2.3.3 Analytical Approach

Unobserved heterogeneity may be an issue considering that our data contain multiple observations per VC firm. In addition, the measure of network cohesion may be potentially endogenous. In order to address these concerns, we use the panel Hausman–Taylor regression model (Hausman and Taylor 1981). This approach offers two important benefits. Similar to a fixed-effects model, it accounts for unobserved heterogeneity by allowing for correlation between regressors and the individual VC firm's effects. Yet, contrary to the fixed-effects model, it allows the estimation of regressors that are invariant over time within VC firms (Greene 2003). Furthermore, this method accounts for endogeneity by using both the between and the within variations of the exogenous variables as instruments for the specified endogenous variables (Baltagi 2008). We perform a Hausman postestimation test to ensure that this model is preferable over a panel regression with fixed or random effects. The p-value for the test (0.84) suggests that the Hausman–Taylor estimation is appropriate. Finally, we perform numerous robustness tests including analyses with different model specifications (see below).

Prior to analyzing our data, we standardized all our main variables (*Cohesive network, Maturity*, and *Status*) around the Z-score to avoid high inter-item correlations among the interaction terms (Gao et al. 2010). After this standardization, we created two- and three-way interaction terms to test our hypotheses following Friedrich (1982). Finally, in line with the three-way interaction methodology discussed in Aiken and West (1991), we also included a Maturity $\times$ Status interaction term.

2.4   Results

Table 2.1 provides descriptive statistics and correlations. Table 2.1 shows that the average amount of *Co-investors* is about four, that about 50 percent of the VCs were UK based, with further 25 percent being from the U. S. In addition, about two-thirds of VCs are independent as opposed to captives. The average Herfindahl index is 0.75, indicating that VCs in our study are mostly specialized. On average, about £12B have been invested each year in the UK. To ensure that multicollinearity is not an issue, we conduct a VIF test and all the variables are within the acceptable limit of 10 (Kutner et al. 2004), with the average VIF being 2.21.

Table 2.2 reports the results of the Hausman–Taylor panel regression. At the first step, we include controls only. Not surprisingly, *VC experience* significantly increases the amount of exits. Similarly, the effect of amount of *Funds Under Management* is significant and positive. *Competition* (e.g., the amount of capital invested annually) increases performance and this could be explained by the fact that new firms enter the market in boom times (Gompers et al. 2008). The VC firm's maturity and status individually increase performance, and their interaction effect is positive. Most importantly, the *Network Cohesion* measure shows no significant direct relationship with performance. The lack of significance strengthens our main argument that the effects of the syndication network structure on performance should not be considered in isolation from the two contingency factors.

In the second step, we include an interaction between our proxy of network cohesion and firm maturity to test hypothesis 1, which suggests a negative effect of this interaction on VC firm performance. Indeed, the interaction variable's coefficient is negative and highly significant ($p < .05$), in line with our first hypothesis. This addition also significantly increases the explanatory power of our model (F change = 5.24; $p < .05$). Young firms benefit from having a cohesive network, but once they mature, a structural holes network is preferable.

At step 3, we add the interaction term between cohesion and status. This addition significantly increases the explanatory power of our model (F change = 14.04; $p < .01$). Hypothesis 2 predicts a negative effect of the interaction between a cohesive network and status on performance.

Table 2.1 Descriptive statistics and Pearson correlations

	Variable	Mean (S.D.)	1	2	3	4	5	6
1	VC Performance (Exits)	0.11(0.45)						
2	P.E. Investors Dummy	0.62(0.48)	0.06*					
3	Funds Under Management	6.79(11.81)	0.14*	0.11*				
4	Co-investors	3.82(2.74)	0.00	-0.02	0.01			
5	Venture age at Financing	29.5(17.79)	-0.02	-0.04*	-0.00	-0.17*		
6	US fund	0.25(0.44)	-0.03*	0.03*	0.20*	0.09*	-0.02	
7	Non-UK Locations Fund	0.24(0.43)	-0.07*	0.02*	-0.05*	0.06*	-0.02	-0.32*
8	VC experence	2.96(7.77)	0.51*	0.09*	0.20*	-0.03*	-0.00	-0.10*
9	Investment Diversifications	0.75(0.29)	-0.19*	0.03*	-0.19*	0.04*	0.02	0.21*
10	Compctition	12257(7400)	0.08*	0.00	-0.01	-0.07*	0.09*	-0.04*
11	LSE	50.36(191.21)	-0.01	0.00	-0.01	0.00	-0.02*	-0.00
12	Network cohesion	0(1)	0.04*	-0.01	0.00	0.15*	0.01	-0.00
13	Status	0(1)	0.16*	0.03*	0.06*	0.15*	-0.01	-0.06*
14	Maturity	0(1)	0.12*	0.02	29*	0.13*	0.04*	0.17*
15	Maturity X Status	0.07(1.03)	0.11*	0.01	0.02	0.03*	0.02	-0.05*
16	Network cohesion X Maturity	0.07(1.00)	-0.03*	-0.01	-0.02*	-0.02	0.03*	-0.01
17	Network cohesion X Status	0.17(0.7)	-0.09*	-0.01	-0.03*	0.12*	-0.01	-0.01
18	Net. cohesion X Maturity X Status	0.00(0.74)	-0.07*	-0.02	0.02	0.12*	0.01	0.01

$n = 5{,}015$. *denotes significance at 5 percent level or better.

7	8	9	10	11	12	13	14	15	16	17
-0.12*										
0.22*	-0.36*									
-0.03*	0.13*	-0.05*								
0.01	-0.02*	0.03*	-0.12*							
-0.03*	0.08*	-0.14*	-0.02*	0.03*						
-0.05*	0.24*	-0.17*	-0.11*	0.02	0.17*					
-0.09*	0.18*	-0.17*	0.20*	-0.05*	0.07*	0.06*				
-0.01	0.17*	-0.01	-0.07*	0.01	0.00	0.41*	0.00			
0.02	-0.00	-0.00	-0.05*	-0.00	0.03*	0.00	-0.02	0.18*		
-0.03*	-0.13*	-0.00	-0.08*	-0.00	-0.00	0.35*	0.00	-0.02	-0.00	
-0.00	-0.08*	0.00	0.02	0.00	0.01	-0.01	0.25*	0.29*	0.02	0.22*

Table 2.2 *Hausman–Taylor longitudinal regression and GLS with random effects*

	DV: VC performance (Exits)				
Controls	Model 1 Hausman–Taylor	Model 2 Hausman–Taylor	Model 3 Hausman–Taylor	Model 4 Hausman–Taylor	Model 5 GLS random
P. E. Investors dummy funds under	0.016 (0.012)	0.016 (0.012)	0.016 (0.012)	0.015 (0.012)	0.015 (0.00)
Management	0.001* (0.001)	0.001* (0.001)	0.001* (0.001)	0.001* (0.001)	0.001 (0.001)
Co-investors	0.002 (0.002)	0.002 (0.002)	0.003 (0.002)	0.003 (0.002)	0.004**(0.00)
Venture age at financing	0.000 (0.000)	0.000 (0.000)	0.000 (0.000)	0.000 (0.000)	-0.000*(0.00)
U.S. fund	0.009 (0.015)	0.009 (0.015)	0.007 (0.015)	0.005 (0.015)	0.005 (0.01)
Non-UK locations fund	-0.003 (0.015)	-0.002 (0.015)	-0.006 (0.015)	-0.006 (0.015)	-0.007 (0.01)
VC experience[b] Investment	0.029** (0.001)	0.029** (0.001)	0.028** (0.001)	0.028** (0.001)	0.027** (0.00)
Diversification	-0.004 (0.023)	-0.006 (0.023)	-0.005 (0.023)	-0.007 (0.023)	-0.008 (0.02)
Competition	0.000* (0.000)	0.000[†] (0.000)	0.000[†] (0.000)	0.000[†] (0.000)	0.000[†] (0.000)
LSE	0.000 (0.000)	0.000 (0.000)	0.000 (0.000)	0.000 (0.000)	0.000 (0.00)
Network cohesion[ab]	-0.006 (0.007)	-0.004 (0.007)	-0.006 (0.007)	-0.004 (0.007)	-0.005 (0.00)
Maturity[b]	0.007 (0.006)	0.006 (0.006)	0.007 (0.006)	0.013* (0.006)	0.014* (0.00)
Status[b]	0.015* (0.006)	0.014* (0.007)	0.026** (0.007)	0.019** (0.008)	0.017* (0.00)
Maturity × status[b]	0.007 (0.006)	0.010 (0.006)	0.005 (0.006)	0.014* (0.007)	0.014* (0.00)

DV: VC performance (Exits)					
Controls	Model 1 Hausman–Taylor	Model 2 Hausman–Taylor	Model 3 Hausman–Taylor	Model 4 Hausman–Taylor	Model 5 GLS random
2-way Interaction Hypotheses					
Network cohesion ×		-0.012* (0.006)	-0.011* (0.006)	-0.012* (0.006)	-0.014** (0.00)
Maturity (H1) Network cohesion ×			-0.036** (0.009)	-0.026** (0.009)	-0.025* (0.01)
Status (H2)					
3-way Interaction Hypothesis					
Maturity × Network cohension × Status (H3)				-0.028** (0.009)	-0.027** (0.01)
Constant	-0.004 (0.025)	-0.001 (0.025)	0.008 (0.025)	0.006 (0.025)	0.008 (0.02)
Wald-Chi square	1804.48**	1810.03**	1830.9**	1843.99**	606.31**

$p < 0.1^{\dagger}, p < 0.05^{*}, p < 0.01^{**}$.

The Wald-Chi square statistic refers to the random-effect model, while the F statistics to the fixed-effects model.

[a] When this measure is high, the focal VC firm is adopting a cohesive strategy, while when it is low it is adopting a brokerage strategy. In the Hausman–Taylor regression, this measure is considered endogenous.

[b] This measure has been centered around the Z-score to avoid collinearity issues with the interaction term.

Supporting this hypothesis, the two-way interaction is negative and highly significant ($p < .001$).

Finally, at step 4, we enter the three-way interaction term to test hypothesis 3. The addition of this variable significantly increases the significance of our model (F change $= 8.38$; $p < .01$) suggesting that there is a strong interplay among syndication network structure and the firm's maturity and status in terms of their performance outcomes. Supporting hypothesis 3, the three-way interaction term is negative and highly significant ($p < .01$). A negative sign indicates that a status and maturity, taken together, reinforce the benefits of a structural holes position.

To help further interpretation of our results, we plot the three interactions in Figure 2.1.

Figure 2.1a shows that firm's maturity has a strong impact on the relationship between network structure and performance. A cohesive network exerts a positive influence on performance of younger firms, whereas a network rich in structural holes is beneficial to more mature firms. Figure 2.1b illustrates the moderation effect of status. A cohesive network has a positive effect on the performance of lower-status firms. On the other hand, a network with structural holes is beneficial to higher-status firms. It is interesting to note that, for both moderations, a cohesive network evens out the advantages stemming from maturity and status. Finally, Figure 2.1c illustrates the joint moderation effect of maturity and status. A structural holes network is particularly supportive to performance of mature and high-status firms. Therefore, more mature firms will have better performance in a structural holes network, but even more so when the maturity is combined with high status. Interestingly, all three interactions are disordinal in form (Lubin 1961). The graphs show that for high levels of maturity and status the positive effect of network cohesion on performance is not only reduced but also reversed to negative.

2.4.1 Robustness Tests

In order to confirm the robustness of our findings, we performed several additional tests using different estimation methods and variable operationalizations. First, we used a panel regression with standard errors clustered around the focal VC firm with fixed and random effects as an alternative

Fig. 2a The effect of firm's maturity on the network structure–performance relationship

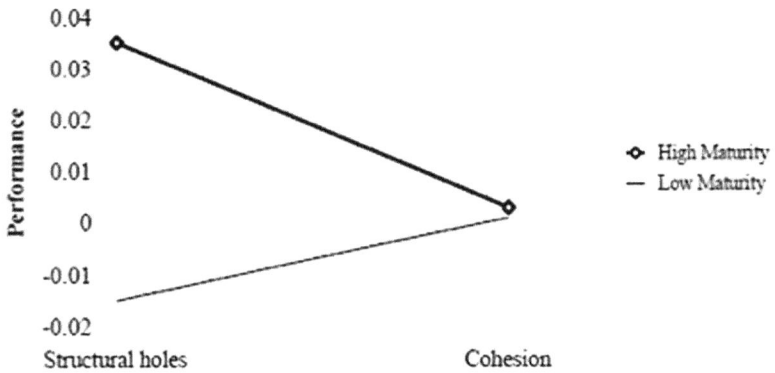

Fig. 2b The effect of firm's status on the network structure–performance relationship

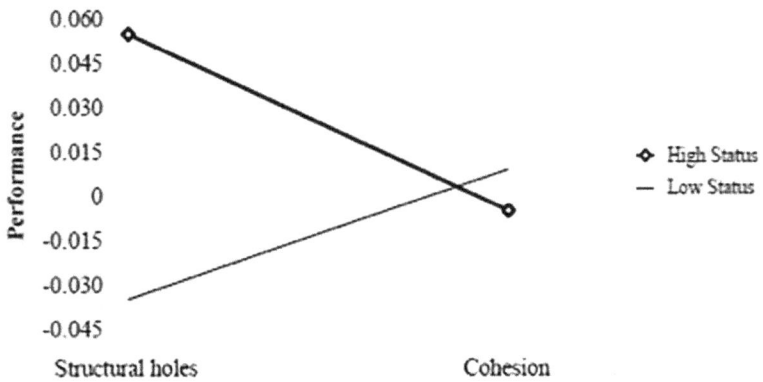

Fig. 2c The joint effect of firm's status and maturity on the network structure–performance relationship

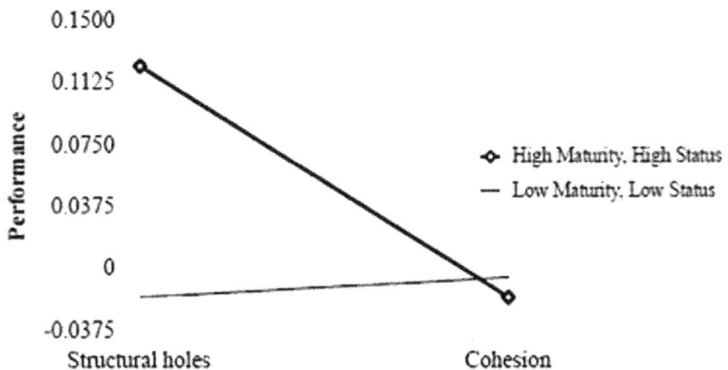

Figure 2.1 Graphical representation of the main effects

regression tests to verify our results. We also tested our hypotheses using a random-effects negative binomial regression. In addition, we re-run our analyses with different operationalizations of our maturity variable using a binary 6 and 10 year cut-off variables similar to Gompers (1996), as well as 6 and 10 year maturity thresholds for the three stages of maturity. In all these analyses, the results were qualitatively similar to our main findings. Finally, considering that during the early stages a VC firm might have a problem with developing a network, we restricted our analyses to firms with at least one connection. We run both Hausman–Taylor models as well as both random and fixed effects. The reduction in observations reduced significance levels but results remain constant.

Furthermore, although the Hausman–Taylor model is appropriate for endogenous variables, we conducted additional endogeneity tests. Following Shipilov (2006), we performed sensitivity analyses to determine whether or not VC performance affects the network structure by reversing the causality of our arguments. We tested this reverse causality by using a system of simultaneous equations following Baum and Haveman (1997). In the first equation, the VC's performance was regressed on its network structure, maturity, and status. In the second equation, the VC's network structure was regressed on its performance, status, and maturity. 3SLS regression analysis does not suggest that VC's performance, status, or maturity affect network structure. In similar analyses, we do not find that the VC's present high-quality investments (considered as present investments with future exits) affect network structure.

2.5   Discussion

In this study, we extend the network and entrepreneurial finance literatures by arguing that the effects of VC investment network structure on the performance of an individual VC are contingent upon the resource endowment of the focal firm. We build on previous research arguing that network cohesion has both advantages and disadvantages (Kilduff and Brass 2010), and we propose two contingencies related to the firm's resources: the VC firm's maturity and status. We find that the resource endowment has negative impact on benefits arising from a cohesive network. Specifically, membership in a cohesive network creates performance advantages for a young and low-status VC, but at the same time negatively impacts performance of a mature and high-status VC. Younger firms have low internal resources and therefore need to tap into their partners' expertise readily available in a cohesive network. On the contrary, more mature VC firms in a cohesive network would receive redundant resources and face limits on their flexibility. In addition, status is an important way to attract external resources. Higher-status firms are more frequently invited to co-invest in quality deals and are able to act as brokers. Therefore, in a structural holes network, status will positively moderate the network–performance relationship.

Finally, we propose that maturity and status reinforce each other in terms of providing moderating effects on the relationship between network cohesion and performance. Although maturity helps to discover promising start-ups and support their development, high status is needed to be invited to participate in the investment syndicates.

Our theory and evidence advance prior research in both network and entrepreneurial finance in several ways. First, we contribute to a broader network research which mainly considered externality effects associated with resources available to the focal firm through the network. We complement previous work by accounting for the firm's resource needs, contingent upon its characteristics. We consider two factors that affect these needs: the firm's maturity and status. Taking into account both the supply and the demand for resources in a network is an important contribution to network theory which currently lacks a resource-based view of social capital (Lavie 2006; Oh et al. 2004).

Second, we utilize our resource-based approach to the network research to contribute to the intense and important debate about the effects of network cohesion on firm performance (Burt 1992; Coleman 1998). To explain inconsistent findings (Echols and Tsai 2005), the literature suggests that both cohesion and structural holes can be advantageous under different conditions (Burt 2001; Kilduff and Brass 2010). Scholars have tested moderators which fall under three broad categories, namely network context (e.g., Baum et al. 2012), change in the environment (e.g., Gargiulo and Benassi 2000), and business strategy (e.g., Shipilov 2006). We extend this literature by suggesting and analyzing two additional potential factors that may tip the cost–benefit trade-offs associated with network structural characteristics, namely firm maturity and status.

Third, we contribute to the entrepreneurial finance literature. Previous studies highlighted both the positive (Bygrave 1988; Hochberg et al. 2007; Lerner 1994) and negative (Filatotchev et al. 2006; Steier and Greenwood 1995; Wright and Lockett 2003) effects of financial syndication. We demonstrate that network structure in which a specific deal is embedded has a strong impact on exit outcomes. Therefore, it is important for VCs to consider carefully their choice of partners in conjunction with their own resources when syndicating a deal because this may generate different networks that contribute differently to their performance. In this regard, we answer the call for a "more fine-grained analysis of how the external networks brought by the VC impact portfolio company performance" (Manigart and Wright 2014: 80).

2.6   Limitations and Directions for Future Research

This study is not without limitations. First, our focus is on formal VC firm networks associated with co-investing with other VCs. This approach has been widely used in previous research because of its focus on information exchange and investment collaboration (Hochberg et al. 2007, 2010). Furthermore, this method provides a clear track of each interaction among network members. However, it also creates two potential drawbacks that can offer interesting avenues for future research.

First, syndication does not capture all the exchange of information among VCs, which could also come from informal, personal networks of managers, or networks arising from being part of industry associations. Therefore, it would be interesting to consider the interaction between individuals and their firms within a multiplex network study. For example, what is the impact of network structure on a young VC firm but with experienced management? Similarly, can managers' status compensate for the lack of industry legitimacy of the VC firm?

Another level of analysis that may offer interesting insights is the syndicate itself. Bringing together analysis of VC syndicate with research on alliances (Wassmer 2010) can help to address important research questions such as: Which syndicates perform better? What is the best syndicate composition? What is the effect of the syndicate's combined social capital on performance of its members?

Although we consider resource needs of the firms, we do not research the types of partners a firm chooses but rather the network it is embedded in. Research examining inter-firm exchange relationships suggests that firms gain status by forming relationships with high-status firms and lose status through relationships with low-status firms (Chung et al. 2000; Podolny 1994). An interesting study would try to understand when a high-status firm, for example, partners with a low-status partner, and in what type of network.

Furthermore, we look at VC industry in one country. We make this choice deliberately, to ensure consistency in our sample and avoid bias due to macro-economic differences such as legal and regulatory factors. However, Chaline et al. (2012) provide evidence of significant institutional differences of VC industry across various countries. For example, the UK investment industry is characterized by a complex web of contractual, social, and political relations centered within the City of London. Future studies should test our results in different institutional settings (industries and countries) to confirm our findings.

Finally, we consider the interrelation between the firm's resources and network structure, assuming that the firm's partners are homogeneous. Future research might try to understand the interplay between the focal firm attributes, the network structure, and the alter's attributes. For example, a study by Ma et al. (2013) looks at how power and status mismatch may impact the effectiveness of a syndicate. Finally, future research should consider the interplay of other organizational contingencies, such as types of VCs, with network cohesion in terms of organizational outcomes.

2.7   Conclusions

We build on the idea that VC syndicates are investment networks that provide resources to the focal VC firm. We theorize that the advantages stemming from a particular network structure are contingent upon resources controlled by the firm. We show that mature and high-status VCs benefit less from network cohesion. We believe that future research bringing together the resource-based view of the firm and network theory has the potential to make important further inroads in terms of our understanding of how networks affect their member firms.

CHAPTER 3

Does Familiarity among Venture Capital Co-Investors Lead to Higher Performance?

Venture capital (VC) firms repeatedly establish co-investment alliances, namely syndicates. Yet, although the practice of partnering with the same partners over time is widely adopted in the industry, we do not know what is the impact of repeated transactions (i.e., familiarity) on syndicate performance. We build upon alliance literature (e.g., Gulati 1995a, 1995b) that highlighted the importance of familiar alliance partners but did not fully investigate its impact on alliance performance. The few empirical papers going into this direction showed contradictory results. By theorizing that the relationship between familiarity and performance is curvilinear, we try to reconcile these findings. Familiarity has the potential to reduce syndicate conflicts but at the same time it limits the uniqueness of the resources available. Furthermore, we propose that the effect of familiarity is contingent on the nature of the previous interactions, as well as on contextual factors such as start-up age and VC industry development. We build our theoretical hypothesis supported by interviews with practitioners and test them with a comprehensive database of 36,155 the U.S. VC investment (1980–2013) in the biotech and medical industries. We offer strategic advice to both entrepreneurs and VCs.

3.1 Introduction

VC syndicates are a form of interfirm alliances that received considerable attention in both the VC and alliance literature (Wright and Lockett 2003).

A VC syndicate arises when a group of investors jointly provide equity capital to a start-up under conditions of uncertainty, and payoffs are subsequently shared among them (Lerner 1994). This practice is not only very common (Jääskeläinen et al. 2006; Jääskeläinen 2012) but it also impacts the likelihood of achieving a successful exit (Brander et al. 2002). The choice of syndicate partners, though, is not random (Gulati 1995a, 1995b). VC firms tend to choose the same co-investors over time creating a familiar and cohesive network (Bygrave 1987, 1988). A VC manager we interviewed told us: "the co-investors I like working with are the ones I tend to stick to going forward." Similarly, various authors (e.g., Hochberg et al. 2007; Lerner 1994) found that VCs reciprocally invite each other to investments opportunities. However, although various alliance scholars (e.g., Gulati 1999) highlighted the importance of familiarity and repeated transactions on the functioning of an alliance, this has not been investigated in co-investment alliances such as the VC syndicates.

This paper intends to fill this gap in the entrepreneurship literature and to contribute to the alliance literature by deepening our understanding of the impact of partners' familiarity on co-investment alliances' performance. In doing so, we answer a recent call to investigate under which circumstances syndicate relationships lead to improved performance (Hopp 2009; Manigart and Wright 2014). Previous studies found both positive (Brander et al. 2002; Cumming and Walz 2010), neutral, or negative (Meuleman et al. 2009; Hege et al. 2006; Dimov and De Clercq 2006) relationships between syndication and performance.

Although it has been acknowledged three decades ago that VC syndicates generate familiar groups (Bygrave 1987, 1988), to the best of our knowledge, this is the first study that tests the impact of repeated transactions (e.g., familiarity) on VC syndicate performance. In fact, despite the importance of understanding the impact of syndicate and alliance composition (Hoffmann 2007), we are not clear about the amount of alliance familiarity that leads to superior performance.

Prior research has suggested that VCs enter into syndicates to access complementary resources (Hopp 2009) to support the growth of the investee company. For example, a VC might have relevant expertise on certain technologies but have limited knowledge of foreign markets, and it might find beneficial to partner with an investor that knows little about technology but has international experience. Yet, by partnering with other investors, significant agency risks and coordination costs might arise (Filatotchev et al. 2006; Steier and Greenwood 1995; Wright and Lockett 2003).

In order to reduce possible conflicts, VC firms have the tendency to co-invest with the same partners over time (Bygrave 1987, 1988). By doing so, VCs learn about each others' competences, skills, and develop trust (Shapiro et al. 1992). Yet, although repeatedly co-investing with the same partners engenders trust and reduces conflicts, it also limits the uniqueness of the resource available within the investment alliance.

Notwithstanding the importance of familiarity and trust, an investment alliance should not only aim to reduce its costs, conflicts, and complexity, but also access diverse information and capabilities (Baum et al. 2000: 270). The composition of an alliance should not only be the product of an effort to reduce uncertainty, but also to assemble valuable skills and resources (Baker 1990; Burgers et al. 1993). In this regard, although familiarity reduces risks such as agency and coordination costs, free riding, and opportunism, it also reduces the information and resource diversity available within the alliance (Burt 1992, 2001). When an alliance is composed by familiar firms, the pool of resources and information available tends to be redundant and therefore of lower value. In the previous example, if the two VCs repeatedly invest together, they are both likely to develop an understanding of the technology and the foreign markets they are dealing with; hence, their resource advantage to co-invest fades away. In sum, by repeatedly co-investing together, VCs establish trust but their resources become duplicative and therefore the combined value will decrease in the long term.

Previous alliance studies implicitly argued that familiarity is positive for alliance performance (Gulati 1999; Gulati and Gargiulo 1999). Yet, empirical results identified both a negative (Goerzen 2007) and a positive (Zollo et al. 2002) relationship between familiarity and performance. Hence, we first try to unravel these competing effects of familiarity on syndicate performance. We propose that familiarity can have both a positive and a negative impact on performance, and therefore we test the curvilinear effect of familiarity on syndicate performance.

In addition, departing from previous studies that assumed that familiarity is homogeneous and independent (e.g., Gulati 1995a, 1999), we propose that the performance effect of familiarity is contingent on both the nature of previous interactions and contextual factors. Thus, we distinguish between successful (arising from positive past interactions) and non-successful familiarity. In the VC industry, a large portion of VC investments fails or can be considered "living dead" (Ruhnka et al. 1992). Moreover, applying an agency and resource-based view lens, we consider the contingent effects of the age of the start-up and the development stage of the VC industry. We propose that the younger the start-up, the more exacerbated the agency costs among investment partners and the more the investee company needs non-duplicative resources; In addition, in a developed VC industry, the competition for resources is stronger and the need for specialized inputs more relevant. Therefore these two factors moderate the relationship between syndicate familiarity and performance.

We test our hypotheses in the context of the U.S. VC syndicates with a comprehensive dataset of VC syndicates from 1980 to 2013. Our theory is complemented by interviews with industry experts. We study the effect of familiarity on the performance of the syndicate alliances, namely the achievement of a successful exit through an Initial Public Offering.

3.2   VC Syndicates and Performance

VC firms invest in start-ups that have the potential to increase in value and release capital at the time of a successful exit. In line with previous studies (for a review, see Manigart and Wright 2014), our measure of syndicate success is represented by a listing on the stock market of the investee company. A relevant portion of the VC investments is conducted through co-investment syndicate alliances (Manigart et al. 2006). In the VC market, there is a multitude of reasons that can explain the syndication of deals (e.g., better selection, improved monitoring, value adding) but, nevertheless, syndicates represent a long-term commitments in which the participating firms exchange knowledge, resources, and skills (Bygrave 1987; De Clercq and Dimov 2008; Wright and Lockett 2003). Simply put, firms form co-investment alliances when they need additional resources (Dimov and Milanov 2010). A VC we interviewed told us: "another advantage [of syndication] is that various investors provide different value adding activities and it is important to bring in co-investors that complement your value/skills/core competency to ensure that your portfolio company receives the optimal value it can get to both mitigate/ eliminate risks and also accelerate growth." Examples of resources can be represented by technology expertise, contacts, capital, market knowledge, or simply time availability. Yet, in order for the resources to add value to the syndicate, they need to be unique rather than overlapping. Our interviewee mentioned "different" and "complementary." Therefore, if investors A and B possess the same resources, the combination of the two is not likely to add more value to the start-up than A or B separately. Rather, a joint investment from A and B is likely to increase the agency costs compared to a solo-investor situation.

Although we may imagine that VCs have the common goal to financially develop the investee company, VCs differ so do their incentives and objectives. A VC investor manager mentioned that VC firms differ in terms of culture, philosophy, strategy, and interests. Various researchers (Mäkelä and Maula 2006; Fried and Hisrich 1995; Wright and Lockett 2003) stressed the agency costs involved in VC syndicates. Filatotchev et al. (2006) and Meuleman et al. (2009) introduced the principal– principal conflict that hinders the performance of the syndicate. Adding more partners to a syndicate leads to bureaucracy (Steier and Greenwood 1995), complex managerial issues, and dilution of ownership (Wright and Lockett 2003) which could incentivize free riding (Dimov and De Clercq 2006).[1] In fact, a VC investor mentioned that: "[a risk] that can be avoided but may sometime arise, is having too many investors influencing the portfolio companies' strategy, which could be disastrous. This is why it is critical that investors are aligned form the start (alignment of interests). Other scenarios in which conflicts could arise are mergers and acquisitions, entry of new investors, company strategy

---

[1]It is important to note that the extant literature highlighted four types of conflicts are present in the VC model: (a) between the start-up founders and the VCs, (b) among the various VCs involved in a syndicate, (c) among the various founders of each start-up, (d) between the VCs (general partners) and the limited partners. We focus on the conflict among VCs co-investing together in a syndicate.

(particularly during a pivot, or strategy change), when performance is not up to par. Basically, every time that a potential downside risk arises, there is potential for a conflict between co-investors." Similar findings appear in the alliance literature that suggests that the costs of interfirm collaboration increase substantially with more partners (Artz and Brush 2000; Parkhe 1993).

Although conflicts can arise in any situation, conflicts among co-investors are likely to be reduced when the investors are familiar with each other. A VC manager that we interviewed mentioned that: "certainly, working with credible, reputable, co-investors that you've worked with in the past is the best way to mitigate such conflicts. [. . .]. You have to know a lot about your co-investors before you jump in. Normally, the co-investors I like working with are the ones I tend to stick to going forward. Track records are the best indication how high or low the potential of conflicts with a particular co-investor might be." Another investor told us that: "it is never about VC vs. VC, it is more of who do I know well enough that I can work with together [. . .]. If I was in Kleiner, and you were in Sequoia,[2] most likely I would call you first for a good deal because I know you so well and we are friends." Similarly, Gulati (1995b) showed that partners' familiarity reduces uncertainty about the partner's behavior and reduces conflicts. Therefore, based on empirical as well as theoretical evidence (Grewal et al. 2006), we argue that familiarity (e.g., repeated interactions) reduces conflicts between co-investors.

At the same time, familiarity decreases the potential to add value to the start-up since the various investors' know each other and their resources tend to be overlapping. If two firms repeatedly partner with each other, they are more likely to develop a common-redundant set of skills, resources, and contacts (Burt 1992). Hence, the impact of familiarity on syndicate performance presents a trade-off. In order to disentangle this trade-off, we propose three factors shape the balance between familiarity and performance in this context. The agency issues involved in a syndicate and the value of unique resources are contingent on three factors: the nature of familiarity, the development stage of the investee firm and of the industry.

---

[2]Kleiner (KPCB) and Sequoia Capital are well-known international VCs.

3.3   Theory and Hypotheses

Baum et al. (2000: 270) help us to explain the trade-off offered by syndicate familiarity: a co-investment alliance is efficiently configured when it provides "access to more diverse information and capabilities per alliance, and thus produce[s] desired benefits with minimum costs of redundancy, conflict, and complexity." We propose that familiarity reduces not only complexities and conflicts, but also information and capabilities' uniqueness. Hence, we adopt a contingency approach to explain under which circumstances one or the other aspects of familiarity will be dominant. In order to extrapolate the contingency nature of familiarity, we first hypothesize on its direct effect on performance and subsequently we include three contingencies.

3.3.1 Familiarity and Performance

The underlying mechanism of familiarity is that, through repeated partnerships, VC firms develop a greater understanding of each other's needs, capabilities, and discover opportunities for new alliances and this loop leads to even greater familiarity. Repeated transactions help alliance partners to develop and reinforce interorganizational routines that are repetitive patterns of interdependent actions (Dionysiou and Tsoukas 2013; Feldman and Pentland 2003). Through repeated interactions, actors develop norms guiding their interactions and a shared understanding that facilitates resource exchange in general, and the transfer of knowledge and information in particular (Uzzi 1997). Repeated interactions allow partner firms to better understand their own behaviors and to identify best practices for joint activities and contexts (Dionysiou and Tsoukas 2013; Faems et al. 2012). Firms that form repeated collaborations often develop structural arrangements that have been proved to be an effective and efficient alliance management approach (Kale et al. 2002) and are likely to understand each other's knowledge stock (Gino et al. 2010). In the VC industry, repeated co-investments generate routinized procedures to conduct due diligences, structure term sheets, run board meetings, and manage the investment alliance. For example, the conflicts that might arise while writing a term sheet, after the first co-investment where a term sheet is agreed upon, will probably be softened on subsequent investments.

This reciprocal knowledge and mutual understanding engender rising trust between firms that appears to reduce agency costs within the alliance (Goerzen 2007; Gulati 1995a, 1995b). Gulati (1999) explains that familiarity reduces the uncertainty related to partner's skills and cooperation, and therefore partners are more likely to choose the same co-investors over time due to lower search costs and alleviated opportunistic behaviors. Familiarity increases the willingness to cooperate and therefore, by lowering agency costs, leads to higher performance (Coleman 1988). A VC investment manager that we interviewed explained that: "from a micro standpoint, mutual knowledge definitely helps to prevent [objective] mismatch and reduce [Subjective/relational] mismatch." Consequently, by lowering possible frictions and agency risks, familiarity creates a collaborative environment within the alliance that in turn will lead to higher performance.

However, while familiarity might help to boost performance by reducing conflicts and improving coordination among partners, there is a risk of over-familiarity. First, as Semrau and Werner (2014) suggest, although repeated interactions might have a significant impact on resource access at the beginning, the marginal benefits of additional co-investments will diminish. At some point, partners are already motivated enough to grant access to the resources they possess, which means that any further partnership will not have an additional effect. Similarly, when working routines and shared norms of understanding are already well established and resource exchange is already very efficient, additional time spent on that specific relationship will not have an added impact on the availability of resources.

Second, familiarity decreases not only conflicts, but also the uniqueness of information and resources available within the co-investment alliance. If partners repeatedly partner with each other, the information and resources they possess is more likely to be redundant (Burt 1992), and therefore of lower value for the syndicate. Along these lines, recent research has demonstrated that repeated alliances can be detrimental to the performance of participating firms. For instance, Goerzen (2007) found that, in a sample of Japanese multinational firms, familiarity with alliance partners led to inferior financial performance. Familiar partners might focus more on common knowledge (Stewart and

Stasser 1995), and the nature of adaptation by repeated partners tends to become incremental (Rosenkopf and Nerkar 2001) and therefore their resources duplicative. Thus, we propose that although initially familiarity decreases the possible frictions arising in a syndicate, more familiarity will have lower benefits on performance and, potentially, too much familiarity might even negatively affect performance. Following this reasoning, we propose a curvilinear effect of familiarity on performance:

H1. Familiarity among alliance partners has an inverse U-shaped relationship with alliance performance.

3.3.2 Familiarity and the Nature of Previous Interactions

Our previous hypothesis is related to repeated interactions, regardless of the outcome of those interactions. However, the influence of a previous interaction on reducing agency costs might have different impacts, if those interactions are successful as opposed to nonsuccessful. An unsuccessful investment might spur doubts about the partners' skills or cooperative effort, and therefore the effect of familiarity on performance will be less positive. Furthermore, previous successes will not only confer information about the partners, but also instill confidence on their cooperation toward a mutual success.

Taking together, it is expected that the proportion of previous successful interactions will have a positive impact on the performance of the syndicate. This reasoning suggests that the inverse U-shaped relationship between syndicate familiarity and performance will peak at higher levels of performance when familiarity is generated by a higher proportion of previous successful interactions.

H2. The proportion of successful interactions moderates the inverted U-shaped relationship between syndicate familiarity and performance in such a way that, at higher proportions of successful interactions, the inverted U-shaped relationship peaks at higher levels of performance.

3.3.3 Familiarity and the Age of the Start-up

A second contingency that has an impact on the advantages and disadvantages of syndicate familiarity is the age of the start-up. The age of a start-up provides a basis for categorizing investments in terms of the uncertainty faced by the VCs at the time of the resource allocation decision. Young start-ups are more risky, more uncertain, and at a higher risk of failure (Matusik and Fitza 2012; Podolny 2001). This leads young start-ups to be endangered by opportunism and free riding among its investors (Dimov and De Clercq 2006) and in a fragile resource position. Hence, syndicates investing in young start-ups benefit from familiarity to reduce agency risks but are harmed by familiarity due to resource redundancy. An interviewee told us that: "younger start-ups are more open to influence, so there could be potential misconduct." Early stage ventures are more uncertain due to uncertified quality, greater demand, technological, resource, and managerial uncertainties (Sapienza et al. 1996; Sapienza and Gupta 1994) and are exposed to a liability of newness (Freeman et al. 1983; Wiklund et al. 2010).

Due to higher uncertainties and risks, the positive effects of familiarity will be strengthened in a younger start-up. A familiar co-investment alliance offers an environment to prevent information asymmetries and it prevents opportunistic behaviors should difficulties arise. Since information asymmetries and uncertainty regarding the best way to develop the venture are present mostly during the early years of a venture, familiarity among co-investors is important to smooth out conflicts in this phase. Casamatta and Haritchabalet (2007) explain that when uncertainty is high (younger start-ups) there is a greater need to gather information about the start-up, and this information is more likely to flow among familiar investment partners that not only have more established communication routines but are also more willing to share information with each other. Organizations benefits from the comfort of relationally familiar partners whenever significant uncertainty looms (Galaskiewicz and Shatin 1981; Podolny 1994; Mizruchi and Stearns 2001; Sorenson and Stuart 2001). In sum, during the early years of the start-up life cycle, where information asymmetries are higher, a syndicate composed of familiar partners, where opportunism is reduced and trust enhanced should lead to higher performance (Coleman 1988). However, an early stage start-up craves for resources to grow and develop itself. A younger start-up necessitates support and inputs from its investors and ideally those inputs are novel and non-duplicative. Hence, the negative effects of familiarity, related to resource redundancy, will be exacerbated in a younger start-up.

On the other hand, older investee companies are less uncertain and more independent from their VC investors. Later-stage start-ups usually need less hands-on coaching (Gupta and Sapienza 1992; Sapienza 1992) and do not require specific technical expertise (De Clercq et al. 2006). Therefore, the effects of investors' familiarity will be milder and less relevant in older companies. An investor mentioned that "[risks of misconduct are] minimized or eliminated as the company grows and builds strong governance." Therefore both the positive and negative effects of familiarity on performance are reduced.

Taking together, it is expected that the impact of syndicate familiarity will be significantly stronger for younger ventures than for older ones that are more independent from investors. Familiarity can decrease the severe agency conflicts arising in younger investee companies but at the same time it limits the resource diversity necessary to develop these firms. This reasoning suggests that the inverse U-shaped relationship between alliance familiarity and performance will be steeper for younger ventures.

H3. The age of the venture moderates the inverted U-shaped relationship between syndicate familiarity and performance in such a way that the inverted U-shaped relationship is steeper in syndicates investing in ventures of young age than in syndicates investing in ventures of old age.

3.3.4 Familiarity and the Development Stage of the VC Industry

Finally, we test the moderating impact of the industry development stage. Mature industries are more competitive and require resource specialization to compete. Syndicates operating in a developed market benefit from familiarity to access resources and limit competition but are harmed by familiarity due to resource redundancy that lowers specialization. On the other hand, less developed industries face higher risk of opportunism as rules and routines are less established.

Murray (1995) argues that VC industry development is likely to be associated with greater competition. As markets become more developed, VC firms are forced to contend deals with greater outside competition (Sapienza et al. 1996). One way to reduce competition and discourage new entrants is to increase barriers to entry and "alliances may be the best way for firms to quickly erect such barriers. [. . .] Because if the objective is to prevent new entrants, it naturally follows that firms are more likely to form more ties with their existing partners [. . .]. Such strategy is more likely since the decrease in uncertainty may indicate a context in which exploitation via strengthening the current network is a more promising strategy than exploration via incorporating new types of partners" (Koka et al. 2006: 729). Tacit collusion, and therefore the possibility to overcome competition, is far easier to sustain in an industry in which the major players are strongly connected with each other (Gulati et al. 2000). Supporting this views, empirical analyses found that tightly connected VC industries experience lower new entries (Hochberg et al. 2010). In sum, we argue that the more an industry develops, the higher the competition will be and therefore the positive effects of familiarity within the syndicate is stronger.

A VC investor explained that "from an industry standpoint, the maturity of a market is a critical environmental component: a mature market with many players (many funds, many start-ups), where deals are 'contendable,' tends toward specialization and common practices." Therefore, in a mature industry, not only there is a higher competition (deals are 'contendable'), but also firms need to be increasingly specialized to succeed. As we previously explained syndicate familiarity reduces resource diversity and if the investors possess duplicative stocks of resources, the amount of specialization within the syndicate is lower leading to negative performance.

On the other hand, a less developed industry will experience lower levels of competition, reduced need for resource specialization and diversity, but higher risk of opportunism. The interviewee mentioned above argued that: "in established markets where you have to compete to get in the best deals, free runners get ruled out quickly; during the early stages of the industry, the opportunities to benefit opportunistically from syndication asymmetries are higher and the negative incentive for the 'free rider' is almost non-existent in the short term." Hence, we expect that in undeveloped industries the main effect of syndicate familiarity on performance will be to strengthen the advantages arising from higher levels of familiarity.

Taking together, it is expected that the impact of syndicate familiarity will be significantly stronger for developed industries than for undeveloped ones, especially with regard to the negative effects. Familiarity will limit the high levels of competition typical of developed industries but at the same time will limit resource diversity and specialization necessary to compete in this environment. Furthermore, it will constrain opportunistic behaviors arising in undeveloped industries. This reasoning suggests that the inverse U-shaped relationship between alliance familiarity and performance will be steeper in developed industries than in undeveloped ones.

H4. The development stage of the VC industry moderates the inverted U-shaped relationship between syndicate familiarity and performance in such a way that the inverted U-shaped relationship is steeper in syndicates investing in a developed industry than in syndicates investing in an undeveloped industry.

3.4   Methods

3.4.1 Data Source and Collection Procedure

The main source for investment data is the Thomson One Banker database that comprehensively reports VC investments worldwide. Our sample is comprised of the U.S. syndicated VC investments from 1980 to 2013 inclusive. Yet, following the VC literature, we cut off the investments at the end of 2008 to allow five years to the investee company to be successful, up to the end of 2013. We restricted our analyses to the biotech and medical industry for two reasons. First, our computational resources would not have allowed us to include investments in more industries for 30 years. Therefore, considering that our hypothesis is time related and focus on the development of relations (familiarity) as well as the start-ups and the industry, we preferred to cover the industry evolution at the expense of other industries. Second, medical and biotech are sectors that require a rather specialized expertise, and therefore it is unlikely that the VCs included invested regularly in other industries, therefore leaving us with numerous missing investments. We include only investments in which both the investor and the start-up are located in the U. S. The rationale for this is that, considering that we take a relational perspective, location is important for relationships to be established and nurtured (Sorenson and Stuart 2001). We also exclude non-VC firms; therefore, we include only "Private Equity Firms," "Private Equity Advisors," or "Fund of Funds." We additionally manually cleaned the data excluding 26 (1.7 percent) investors such as government bodies, foreign investors, and unnamed investors (8.3 percent). This provides us with a final estimation dataset composed by 36,155 investments in 4,604 start-ups by 1,458 VCs. In addition, we conducted interviews with three VC professionals to have a better understanding of the dynamics involved in the process of syndication and its potential conflicts of interest.

3.4.2 Analytical Methods

Since our key dependent variable is a dummy (IPO), we adopted a Heckman Logit two-stage model. This estimation technique fits maximum-likelihood logit models with sample selection. In fact, a potential selection bias might exist in our sample because we only selected syndicated investments, therefore leaving out solo investments. Previous literature has shown that the process of a syndication impacts performance (e.g., Cumming and Walz 2010) and that generally only certain types of deals are syndicated (Manigart et al. 2006). Therefore, we initially ran a Heckman two-stage approach. In the first stage, we regressed the possibility of a start-up to receive VC in a syndicate on previous successes, company and industry development stage, average VC experience, geographical density of VCs active in the metropolitan area, and amount of VC raised in each in year in the metropolitan area. These latter two variables are good instruments as they are less likely to affect the exit potential of a start-up, but are more likely to affect the likelihood of syndicating a deal. Our first-stage regression suggests that both instruments are significantly correlated with the possibility of syndication of a deal but not significantly predicting syndicate success. In the second stage, we ran a logit model to predict the likelihood of the syndicate to achieve a successful exit through an IPO. We included year and area fixed effects and regression random effects.

3.4.3 Measures

Our measures are generally longitudinal and take the syndicate as the unit of analysis.

Performance

Our dependent variable is the success of the syndicate. In line with previous VC literature (Bellavitis et al. 2014; Cumming 2007; Manigart and Wright 2014), we used the capacity of the syndicate to exits its investment in a given year. The IPO measure is the most appropriate to account for the U.S. VC performance (Smith et al. 2011). Once the syndicates reach an IPO, it exits our database.

Syndicate Size

This measure considers the total amount of co-investors in the syndicate as reported on Thomson One Banker. Controlling for syndicate size is relevant to take into account differences in terms of amount of partners, and therefore coordination costs as well as resources' availability.

Syndicate Familiarity

This measure accounts for the familiarity of the syndicate. We first compute the amount of previous dyadic co-investments among pairs and then use the logarithm of this sum. The rationale for this is twofold. First, familiarity resides at the dyadic level. Second, the marginal familiarity decreases with the additional interactions. The difference between co-investing one and two times is clearly higher than between 11 and 12 times. Furthermore, we divide the sum of the logarithms of the dyadic interaction by the logarithm of the total amount of investors in the syndicate. For example, if a syndicate is composed by 4 VCs (A, B, C, and D) and the dyad A-B co-invested in the past three times, while B-C co-invested two times, our measure of familiarity will be as follows: $[\text{Log}(3) + \text{Log}(2)]/\text{Log}(4)$.

Previous Successes

In creating this measure, we have been careful not to incur any collinearity that might arise with the measure of syndicate familiarity. We used the total amount of previous successful interactions, namely previous co-investments exited through an IPO, divided by the amount of previous non-successful interactions. For example, if the members of a syndicate dyadically invested five times together but only two times this dyadic co-investments went through an IPO, this measure will be equal to $2/(5-2)=0.66$. Simply put, if this measure is higher than 1, it means that the syndicate is composed by members whose familiarity is mainly based on success; if lower than 1, mainly based on unsuccessful investments.

Company Age

This measure represents the age of the start-up in years. The older the start-up the more mature it is considered to be. In addition to interacting this measure with familiarity (after standardization) to test H3, this measure is also an important control. It is reasonable to expect that older companies are more likely to be exited.

Industry Development Stage

This measure is based on the reasoning explained by Avnimelech and Teubal (2006). The authors described the VC industry development in Israel and divided it into five phases. Adapting their measure to the U.S. VC industry, we created a categorical measure as follows:

1. Background conditions (from 1980 to 1986): during these years, the U.S. VC industry started to form, take shape, and be legitimized. Levels of investments were still low.
2. Pre-emergence (from 1986 to 1991): during this phase, the amount of investments and players started to grow and the industry formed.
3. Emergence (from 1992 to 2000): these years experienced the boom of the investments fueled by the large amount of opportunities triggered by the advent of the internet.
4. Crisis (from 2001 to 2003 and 2009 to 2010): due to the explosion of the dot-com bubble in 2001, a rapid decline of activity was experienced in the VC industry. Also the latest financial crisis has had a negative impact on the industry in 2009–2010.
5. Consolidation (2003–2009 and 2011 onward). After both crises, the VC industry experienced a period of consolidation where less talented players have been wed out.

Figure 3.1 shows the amount of funds raised in million dollars. Each background trend line represents $80M. Results hold against sensitivity adjustments of the industry development stages.

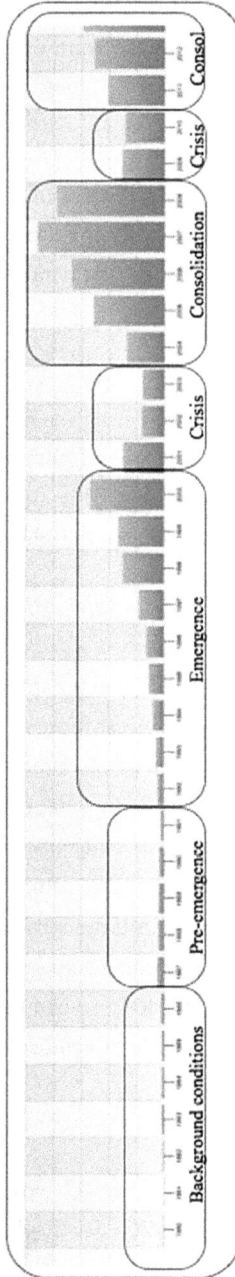

Figure 3.1 Amount of VC funds raised in the U. S. from 1980 to 2013

(Each trend line represents $80M).

Control Variables

In order to rule out alternative explanations and avoid spurious correlations, we will include numerous of controls related to the syndicate, the VC firms involved in each syndicate, the attributes of the portfolio company in which the syndicate invests in, and environmental conditions.

Industry and Area Fixed Effects

We include yearly and area fixed effects to control for macroeconomic differences. The base year is 1980, while the area effects are divided in 25 metro areas as reported in the VC Expert database.

Geographical Density

We control for the amount of active VCs in a given metro area divided by the land area in square miles. Sorenson and Stuart (2008) show that geographical distance matters in choosing VC partners. This measure is one of the two instruments that we implement to control for the selection effect of syndicate.

Amount of Capital Raised in the Area

This measure is the second instrument. When the amount of capital available is greater, VC firms have two choices: invest more capital or invest in more start-ups. The logic of diversification suggests that investing in more firms is needed to spread the risk. Yet, considering that the time available to the VC partners is limited, partnering with other investors is a good strategy to diversify efficiently. In fact, Gorman and Sahlman (1989) found that lead investors visit their investments 1.5 times a month for five hours each time. On the other hand, non-lead venture investors visit the firms less than once a month for about three hours. Hence, when the amount of capital is greater, VC firms can diversify efficiently by syndicating with other firms.

Syndicate Experience

We control for differences in terms of VC experience, precisely the amount of investments made by the VCs involved in the syndicate. This measure is the average of the count of previous investments.

Years from First VC

This measure is a year count from the moment in which the start-up received its first VC investment. With this control, we aim to take into account potential support and coaching received by the firm which is likely to have an impact on the performance of the company.

3.4.3 Results

Table 3.1 reports the descriptive statistics and correlation analyses.

Table 3.2 reports the Heckman selection model. The selected variables have a strong impact in predicting the likelihood of a deal to be syndicated. In particular, our instrumental variables, geographical density and the amount of VC raised, are significant at 0.1 percent levels. Furthermore, the validity of our instruments is confirmed by their non-significant impact on syndicate performance.

Table 3.3 reports the main results. In model 1, we include the controls and the linear measure of familiarity. Among the controls, we find that syndicate size significantly improves performance. Surprisingly, experience has a negative and highly significant impact on performance. This finding might be explained by the fact that experienced VCs tend to have greater amount of capital under management, leading to suboptimal investments. Also, more experienced VCs might have a less flexible and open-minded approach toward investing, and this might be crucial in a dynamic industry such as VC. Finally, start-ups that received investments many years in the past seem to have lost their momentum and might face decreasing possibilities to exit. This might also be explained by having received VC in the early stages, and company age shows that older companies are significantly ($\beta = 0.43$, $p < .001$) more likely to exit.

Furthermore, in model 2, we add the squared measure of familiarity. Results show that familiarity has a significant curvilinear impact on syndicate performance. Although familiarity is initially beneficial ($\beta = 0.39$, $p < .001$), overfamiliarity leads to decreasing performance ($\beta = -0.10$, $p < .01$). These findings provide support for our H1. In models 3–5, we separately add the three contingencies. Model 6 is our full model. Results partially confirm our hypothesis. First, surprisingly the effect of previous success (H2) does not significantly impact performance.

Table 3.1 Descriptive statistics and correlations

	Mean (S.D.)	1	2	3	4	5	6	7	8	9	10	11	12	13	14	15
1	Syndicate performance	0.03(0.16)														
2	Syndicate familiarity	0.06(1.03)	0.04													
3	Familiarity squared	1.06(2.94)	0.01	0.70												
4	Familiarity × Company age	0.08(.91)	-0.01	0.03	-0.06											
5	Familiarity SQ × Company age	0.03(2.17)	0.02	-0.03	-0.17	0.60										
6	Familiarity × Industry dev. stage	0.08(.95)	0.00	0.15	0.15	0.14	0.07									
7	Familiarity SQ × Industry dev. stage	0.15(2.93)	-0.02	0.17	0.21	0.05	0.07	0.63								
8	Familiarity × Previous successes	-0.12(1.73)	-0.01	-0.05	-0.03	-0.06	-0.06	0.00	0.01							
9	Familiarity SQ × Previous successes	-0.09(4.86)	-0.01	-0.06	-0.06	-0.05	-0.07	0.01	0.02	0.91						

Table 3.1 Descriptive statistics and correlations

	Mean (S.D.)	1	2	3	4	5	6	7	8	9	10	11	12	13	14	15
10 Previous successes	-0.02(1.06)	-0.02	-0.11	-0.02	-0.05	-0.05	0.01	-0.00	0.76	0.58						
11 Company age	0(1)	0.04	0.08	0.01	-0.07	0.39	0.00	0.04	-0.03	-0.02	-0.05					
12 Industry development stage	0(1)	-0.06	0.08	0.05	0.00	0.06	-0.05	0.31	0.00	-0.00	0.00	0.15				
13 Syndicate size	0.88(.25)	0.04	0.26	0.11	0.10	0.03	0.03	0.03	-0.05	-0.04	-0.10	0.03	0.03			
14 Syndicate experience	167(149)	0.03	0.20	0.12	-0.01	-0.04	-0.01	-0.04	-0.02	-0.02	-0.04	-0.06	-0.19	0.07		
15 Geographical density	0.04(.01)	0.01	-0.04	-0.03	0.02	0.02	0.01	0.00	-0.00	0.00	0.00	0.03	-0.01	-0.06	-0.03	
16 Years from first VC	3.35(2.93)	0.05	0.26	0.08	0.16	0.31	0.06	0.09	-0.07	-0.05	-0.12	0.58	0.17	0.23	0.01	0.03

N = 21,374; Coefficients equal or above 0.145 are significant at 5 percent levels.

Table 3.2 Heckman two-stage selection model

DV: Deal syndication	
	Model 1
Controls	
Years from first VC	0.11***
	(0.00)
Syndicate experience	0.00***
	(0.00)
Geographical density	-2.64***
	(0.77)
Amount raised in range	0.00***
	(0.00)
Previous successes	-0.05***
	(0.01)
Industry development stage	0.08***
	(0.01)
Company age	-0.09***
	(0.01)
Constant	0.90***
	(0.03)
Lambda	-0.23***
	(0.06)

***p <0.001, **p <0.01, *p <0.05, †p <0.1

In the following sections, we discuss the implications of this finding but, nevertheless, it is interesting to notice that there is no statistically significant difference between growing familiarity out of successes as opposed to non-successful investments. Second, company age significantly moderates the relationship between familiarity and syndicate performance ($\beta = -0.25$, $p < .001$). Also, the second-order interaction term is significant ($\beta = 0.07$, $p < .05$). In particular, confirming our expectations (H3), the age of the investee company significantly shapes the relationship between familiarity and performance. Third, industry development significantly moderates the relationship between familiarity and syndicate performance. Both the first- ($\beta = 0.20$, $p < .05$) and the second-order interaction terms are significant ($\beta = -0.05$, $p < .05$). Statistics lend support to H1, H3, and H4, but not H2.

Table 3.3 Longitudinal logit with random effects and Heckman selection

DV: Syndicate performance (IPO). Standard errors in parenthesis.						
	Model 1	Model 2	Model 3	Model 4	Model 5	Model 6
Controls						
Syndicate size (log)	0.72*** (0.22)	0.66** (0.23)	0.65** (0.23)	0.67** (0.22)	0.64** (0.22)	0.65** (0.21)
Syndicate experience	-0.00** (0.00)	-0.00** (0.00)	-0.00** (0.00)	-0.00** (0.00)	-0.00** (0.00)	-0.00** (0.00)
Geographical density	0.52 (5.65)	0.46 (5.74) (4.27)	0.65 (5.75)	0.02 (5.66)	0.69 (5.65)	0.43 (5.51)
Years from 1st VC	-0.19*** (0.06)	-0.20*** (0.06)	-0.20*** (0.06)	-0.15* (0.06)	-0.22*** (0.06)	-0.17** (0.06)
Inverse mills ratio	-10.48*** (2.15)	-10.68*** (2.22)	-10.71*** (2.23)	-9.45*** (2.20)	-10.97*** (2.18)	-9.57*** (2.13)
Area fixed effects	YES	YES	YES	YES	YES	YES
Year fixed effects	YES	YES	YES	YES	YES	YES
Main variables						
Syndicate familiarity	0.14** (0.04)	0.33*** (0.08)	0.32*** (0.08)	0.34*** (0.08)	0.36*** (0.08)	0.39*** (0.08)
Syndicate familiarity squared		-0.07** (0.02)	-0.07** (0.02)	-0.08** (0.03)	-0.09** (0. 03)	-0.10** (0.03)
Previous successes	0.10[†] (0.06)	0.11[†] (0.06)	0.03 (0.10)	0.10[†] (0.05)	0.12* (0.05)	0.01 (0.09)
Company age	0.56*** (0.09)	0.58*** (0.10)	0.58*** (0.10)	0.44*** (0.10)	0.58*** (0.09)	0.43*** (0.10)
Industry development stage	-0.29 (0.44)	-0.31 (0.44)	-0.32 (0.44)	-0.28 (0.44)	-0.23 (0.44)	-0.19 (0.43)

Continued

Table 3.3 Longitudinal logit with random effects and Heckman selection

DV: Syndicate performance (IPO). Standard errors in parenthesis.						
	Model 1	Model 2	Model 3	Model 4	Model 5	Model 6
Interactions						
Syndicate familiarity × Previous successes			0.10 (0.11)			0.12 (0.11)
Syndicate familiarity SQ × Previous successes			-0.01 (0.03)			-0.02 (0.03)
Syndicate familiarity × Company age				-0.22** (0.07)		-0.25*** (0.07)
Syndicate familiarity SQ × Company age				$0.06^{\dagger}$ (0.03)		0.07* (0.03)
Syndicate familiarity × Industry dev. stage					0.16* (0.07)	0.20** (0.06)
Syndicate familiarity SQ × Industry dev. Stage					$-0.04^{\dagger}$ (0.02)	-0.05* (0.02)
Constant	$-1.63^{\dagger}$ (0.85)	$-1.53^{\dagger}$ (0.86)	$-1.51^{\dagger}$ (0.86)	-1.85* (0.86)	-1.32 (0.85)	$-1.60^{\dagger}$ (0.85)
Log Pseudolikelihood	-2322.14	-2317.15	-2316.59	-2312.4	-2314.4	-2307.56
Wald chi-squared	293.06***	285.87***	285.62***	293.83***	296.51***	312.04***

***$p < 0.001$, **$p < 0.01$, *$p < 0.05$, $^{\dagger}p < 0.1$

To ease the interpretation of our results, we plotted the effects in Figure 3.2. The first graph shows the relationship between familiarity and performance. As predicted, the relationship is represented by an inverted U-shape. Furthermore, although not significant, the proportion of successful interactions shifts the inverted U-shape relationship as predicted in H2. Interestingly, in the last two graphs, I show the moderating effects

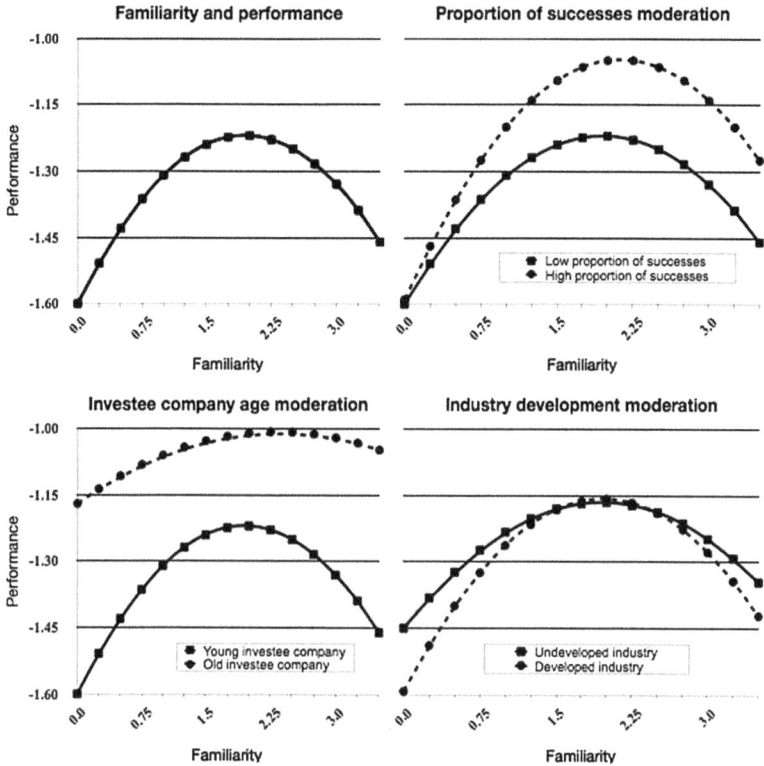

Figure 3.2 The impact of familiarity on performance and moderation effects

of the age of the investee company and the development stage of the VC industry. As hypothesized, the curve is steeper for younger ventures and developed markets.

3.5   Discussion

Does familiarity generated by repeated interactions within a co-investment alliance lead to higher performance? Building on previous alliance literature (e.g., Gulati 1995a, 1995b), we tested the effect of familiarity on VC syndicates' performance. We propose that familiarity generates trust and reduces conflicts but at the same time it reduces the uniqueness of the resources embedded in the alliance. Hence, we suggest a curvilinear effect on performance. In addition, the above relationship must be examined taking into consideration the nature of previous interactions along with contextual factors such as the age of the start-up and development stage of the VC industry. Interestingly, although our proposed contextual factors significantly moderate the relationship familiarity–performance, it looks like there is no significant difference between familiarity generated by previous successes as opposed to non successful interactions.

Contextualizing in the VC industry, we might be able to explain the surprising lack of significance of our findings related to the nature of previous interactions. In our analyses, although the effect is as hypothesized, that is the when familiarity is generated by previous successes familiarity will lead to higher performance (moving the curve upward), this effect is not significant. It is possible that the entrepreneurial mindset typical of the U. S. is considered to be very forgiving toward failures. In addition, the VC industry is sustained by big hits, and failure (or lack of success) is not only accepted and very common, but also considered to be part of the learning process. Along these lines, a VC manager we interviewed mentioned that: "[VC investing] is a gamble. I only made the introduction and told you why you should invest. But in the end the person making the decision is still you and your team." Hence, these cultural aspects might explain the lack of significance of our results. We discuss the generalizability of these findings in the Limitations and Directions for Future Research section.

Our study makes four contributions. First, previous research on the effects of familiarity on alliance performance (Gulati 1999; Gulati 1995a, 1995b; Gulati and Gargiulo 1999; Goerzen 2007; Zollo et al. 2002) theoretically and empirically proposed contradicting arguments. We reconcile these results by showing that familiarity can exert both positive and negative effects on performance. Our models show a statistically strong curvilinear relationship. At the beginning, familiarity reduces conflicts among partners by spurring trust and collaboration, but repeated transactions tend to generate redundant resources that hinder performance. The more two partners co-invest together, the more they will learn about each other and therefore their resources will be redundant and less valuable.

Second, we show that familiarity has to be contextualized. In the VC industry, two important factors are at play: the age of the start-up and the development stage of the VC industry. In younger start-ups, the effects of familiarity are considerable stronger than in older ventures. Syndicates investing in young investee company face high levels of risk and uncertainty and therefore familiarity is able to reduce these risks. However, younger ventures also need resources to survive and grow, and a less familiar syndicate possesses less redundant resources and therefore can add value to the start-up. Even though similar reasonings can be applied to older ventures, these companies are more independent and more established and therefore their performance will be less likely to be impacted by the syndicate composition.

In addition, the impact of syndicate familiarity is stronger in a mature and highly competitive VC industry than in undeveloped VC industry. By repeatedly partnering with the same peers, firms tend to raise barriers to entry and at the same time collaborate to access opportunities which are more "contendable" in a developed market. However, a mature industry requires actors to be specialized and a familiar syndicate, being composed by potentially duplicative sets of resources, is less likely to be specialized, leading the syndicate to lower performance. On the other hand, in an undeveloped industry, there are higher risks of misconduct and a familiar syndicate should reduce potential conflicts. Finally, we also investigate the effect of previous successful interactions. We hypothesized that when two firms have been successful in the past, the familiarity generated by this interaction should offer greater benefits than a previous failure, shifting the curve higher. However, although the effect is in line with our predictions, we find that the nature of previous interactions is not statistically significant. We suggest that this effect is due to the forgiving environment typical of the U. S., where failure is simply part of the game.

Third, our research provides further insights on the benefits and costs of syndication. Previous studies highlighted both the positive (Bygrave 1988; Hochberg et al. 2007; Lerner 1994) and negative (Filatotchev et al. 2006; Steier and Greenwood 1995; Wright and Lockett 2003) effects of syndication on performance. Yet, although it is well known that VCs tend to repeatedly co-invest together spurring familiarity, this phenomenon has not been tested. Generally, those that suggested a positive impact from syndication suggested resource pooling benefits. On the other hand, those suggesting that an increasing number of investors might be detrimental for the start-up emphasized the potential agency risks and coordination costs. We show that familiarity has an impact on both aspects and therefore it is an important characteristic that should be taken into consideration to understand the trade-offs offered by syndication.

Fourth, our study provides insights for practitioners when composing a syndicated. We suggest that a co-investment alliance should be composed taking into consideration the amount of familiarity embedded in the syndicate. This suggests that both entrepreneurs and VC investors should carefully choose their investors and partners. For example, a young start-up might look for investors that know each other and only along its development life cycle delve into different groups, maybe to gain exposure to different expertise that might be useful, for example, to internationalize or enter new markets.

3.6   Limitations and Directions for Future Research

Our study has limitations that hold promise for future research. First, as we previously mentioned, some results might be context specific. Although the VC industry has been recurrently studied in network or alliance studies, it has its peculiarities. For example, we believe that the lack of significance for the nature of previous interactions might be due to the fact that the U.S. VC market is particularly forgiving toward failure that is just deemed as part of the game. Cope (2011: 604) goes further suggesting that failure provides "invaluable insights into the 'pressure points' of the entrepreneurial process, significantly augmenting levels of entrepreneurial preparedness for future enterprising activity." Thus, it would be useful to test our hypotheses in different industries, or simply in different markets. For example, do our findings hold in a developing country? Or in a less entrepreneurial setting?

Limitations aside, future work might explore additional variables and effects. Our paper is one of the first to test the impact of familiarity and its contingencies on performance. Hence, there is room to extend our findings with different measures of performance and moderators. Alternative measures of performance might be survival or innovation output. Alternative moderators that would provide interesting insights might be disruptive or field-changing events. For example, what is the moderating impact of familiarity on the transition from an offline world to an online one? In addition, we considered partners to be homogeneous. It would be interesting to understand for what type of actors is more important to have familiar partners, and with which type of actors is better to be familiar with. Finally, a more fine-grained approach might try to investigate the social benefits of familiarity. It might be that investors and entrepreneurs are willing to forego potential economic benefits in exchange for a pleasant and peaceful environment triggered by familiar partners.

3.7   Conclusion

Does familiarity with co-investors lead to higher syndicate performance? Building on previous research, we propose that familiarity is both beneficial and harmful for performance. We unravel these conflicting effects and propose a curvilinear effect and show that important moderating effects are at play. We reveal the important moderating effects prompted by contextual factors such as the age of the start-up and the development stage of the VC industry to the above relationship. The most significant message from this study is that familiarity is a mixed blessing for performance. An investment alliance must be strategically configured to achieve positive performance by choosing an appropriate mix of partners and considering contextual factors.

CHAPTER 4

Conclusion

This book sheds light on the unresolved questions regarding the impact of venture capital (VC) syndication on performance. Although VC syndicates received considerable attention in the last two decades, still numerous questions remain unanswered. In this book, I conducted a holistic investigation of the conditions under which the benefits of syndicates outweigh the costs. I did so by challenging the homogeneity of syndicates that most studies implicitly assumed. Previous research juxtaposed a syndicated to a non-syndicated deal, or computed the amount of investors and investigated the performance impact. Some studies took a network perspective looking at the centrality or status of VC investors and studied how these impact the performance of the focal VC or start-up. Yet, although these studies offer initial evidence of the effects of syndication on performance, they fail to offer a broader and contextualized picture.

I started by showing that syndicates are a form of inter-firm investment alliance that generates a network of VC firms and start-ups. Building upon network and alliance literatures, I tried to show under what conditions a syndicated deal ought to be preferred over a non-syndicated one. In particular, I show that a number of factors should be considered when making this choice. The first one is related to the type of connections that will be linked to the start-ups within the portfolio. Second, by syndicating deals, VC firms establish networks and the type of network a VC firm is entering into shapes its future performance. Not every VC firm needs the same network and therefore the focal firm should strategically choose what syndicates to enter into, that in turn will impact its overall performance. Third, co-investing generates familiarity among VCs and different level of familiarity have the potential to impact the performance of the syndicate, and therefore of the individual VCs. Hence, VCs should carefully choose what syndicates to enter into, and what partners to invite into the syndicate.

In conclusion, I showed that syndicates are a form of inter-firm alliance that give rise to different levels of social capital. Using different theories, geographical contexts, and unit of analyses I showed that syndicates can be both advantageous and detrimental to the performance of the focal actor. I proposed that VC firms forming syndicates should strategically manage their investment alliances and subsequent networks to achieve positive performance.

This book contributes not only to the VC literature showing the conditions under which syndication leads to better performance, but also to three important debates in the network and alliance literature. The first one is between "structuralist" and "attributist." The former group stresses the relevance of the network structure while the latter calls for more attention on the attributes of a network and its connections. I show that, although the network structure strongly impacts the performance of the focal actor (Chapter 2), the attributes of the partners (Chapter 1), the attributes of the focal firm (Chapter 2), and the composition of the investment alliance through which network structures are generated (Chapter 3) should be considered.

The second debate is related to the trade-off offered by different network structures, and in particular between the researchers advocating the advantages of cohesion and those in favor of structural holes. In Chapter 2, I show that previous network literature focused on the benefits and costs of network structures, but considered the focal firm as exogenous. By relaxing this assumption, I demonstrate that firms possess different resources. Hence, since networks are an important mean to access resources, considering the resource differences of the focal firm is key in explaining the advantages and disadvantages of different network structures. In sum, VC firms rich in internal and external resources should position themselves in a structural holes network, while firms lacking those resources should prefer the social security of a cohesive network.

In relation to the third debate, I tried to add to the alliance literature. Previous alliance studies have shown that firms tend to partner with familiar peers. Yet, the impact of familiarity on performance received limited attention and contradicting evidence. I show that familiarity reduces conflicts of interest but at the same time reduces the diversity of the resources available within the investment alliance. Hence, I propose that familiarity poses a trade-off leading to an inverted U-shaped relation-ship between co-investors familiarity and syndicate performance. Initially familiarity is beneficial, but over-familiarity hampers performance. I also highlight the boundary conditions under which a familiar syndicate boosts the performance of the investment alliance. In particular, the posi-tive and negative effects of familiarity are stronger when the syndicate is investing in a younger start-up and in a mature VC industry. Surprisingly, the nature of familiarity, namely, familiarity generated by successful as opposed to non-successful interactions, does not significantly shape the curvilinear effect.

By looking at these debates, I not only show which contingencies shape the effects of syndication, but also when these contingencies (partners' attributes, network structure, syndicate composition) are more relevant (e.g., in a young start-up, or in a VC with high internal resources). I find that these debates can be resolved by relaxing the assumption of homogeneity and by applying a contingency perspective. Each chapter contributed to a different debate taking a distinct point of view, differ-ent unit of analysis, and geographical contexts. The book investigated networks belonging to start-ups, networks of VCs, and syndicate alliances, in the U. S. and in the UK. Regardless of the context, I showed that by disentangling intrinsic differences within firms, networks, and investment alliances, we are able to explain most empirical contradictions and under-stand when and where syndicates, networks, and investment alliances can be beneficial or detrimental to the performance of the focal actor.

This research not only contributes to entrepreneurship, network, and alliance literature, but also provides strategic guidelines to professionals in the VC industry and other networked industries. I suggest that particular care should be applied in choosing partners that in turn shape the focal firm network structures, and the composition of the investment alliances established. From a start-up point of view, although VC is an important source of finance, a high proportion of VC-backed start-ups fail or lack the traction necessary to achieve an exit. I show that start-ups should approach prospective investors not only considering their capital, status, and potential to add value, but also considering the network that the investors are able to offer. When a start-up receives an investment becomes part of a bigger portfolio. Numerous investors try to put in contact their start-ups and this can be a valuable tool to find new ideas, solutions, and resources. Yet, networking is costly and therefore the types of connections among the portfolio companies should be strategically chosen. Further, considering that start-ups are usually involved in more than one portfolio, they should carefully consider the balance achieved belonging to multiple portfolios.

From a VC firm point of view, syndication offers not only numerous advantages but also costs. I show that a VC firm should consider three factors when structuring their investments and syndicates. First, they need to evaluate their resource endowment as differing resource stocks lead VCs to have different needs. Second, VCs should look at their portfolio as any new investment changes the balance of their portfolios and have the potential to impact the performance of all the other investee companies. For example, they should evaluate an investment not only based on its own merits, but also considering the fit that it might have with other portfolio companies. Third, VCs should be careful in increasing the familiarity with their co-investors as familiarity can be both advantageous and detrimental to their performance. Hence, although it is well known that VC firms tend to repeatedly partner with the same investors over time, this practice poses both advantages and disadvantages.

4.1   Summary of Results

4.1.1 The Effects of Intra- and Extra-industry Networks on Performance of Venture Capital Portfolio Firms

In Chapter 1, looking at the attributes of the portfolio companies' ties, I have shown that not every network connection benefits start-ups in the same way. In particular, I argued that start-up companies are in need of novel resources, and connections in different industries provide original and valuable inputs. In addition, having connections spanning different industries allows to bridge connections and information, therefore gaining brokerage power. However, subsequent analyses showed that the ideal portfolio company's network is composed of both *intra-* and *extra-industry* ties, with the majority of ties being located in different industries.

4.1.2 The Impact of Investment Networks on Venture Capital Firm Performance: A Contingency Framework

In Chapter 2, I investigated the advantages and disadvantages of the network structure arising from syndicates. In particular, I focused on network cohesion and structural holes. Adopting a resource perspective, I have shown that the advantages of each network structure are contingent on the resources controlled by the focal VC firm. Firms with higher resources are better off in a structural holes network that give them brokerage potential, as well as non-redundant new information needed to expand and grow. By contrast, VC firms with lower amounts of resources benefit from the social protection and support of a cohesive network.

4.1.3 Does Familiarity among Venture Capital Co-investors Lead to Higher Performance?

In Chapter 3, I studied the effect of familiarity among co-investment partners on the performance of the syndicate. Although familiarity among VC investors is common, its effect on performance has not been tested yet. I proposed that familiarity is beneficial to reduce agency and coordination costs that endanger the co-investment alliance, but at the same time it reduces the resource uniqueness. Previous studies generally overlooked the effect of familiarity on performance, but the few empirical results available show contradicting evidence. I proposed that these ambiguities can be resolved by considering the nature of previous interactions, the age of the investee company, and the development stage of the VC industry. The curvilinear effect of familiarity within syndicates on performance is strengthened in young and risky start-ups and in developed and competitive industries, while it is weakened in less developed industries but older start-ups. In fact, familiar cohorts have established rules to overcome the typical difficulties and uncertainties arising in an early stage investee company but their familiarity also reduces the uniqueness of the resources available to the start-up; further, familiar syndicates have the potential to limit competition but at the same time their familiarity will reduce the specialization of their resources necessary to compete in a mature industry. Surprisingly, the nature of familiarity does not significantly impact performance.

4.1.4   Limitations and Future Research

A number of limitations apply to this research. First, I focused only on the VC industry. Hence, although this context has been fruitfully used in numerous studies trying to add to network and alliance literature, some of the broader theoretical contributions might not be readily applicable. For example, the impact of familiarity might be stronger in uncertain and dynamic industries such as the VC, but not in more mature and stable industries. Hence, future research might try to extend our results in other industries, and eventually pin point where and how the results do not hold.

Second, within the VC industry I focused on the U.S. and U.K. markets that are the dominant markets. Yet, both markets are developed and with established rules. Hence, my findings might not hold in different countries where sociocultural differences might affect the advantages and disadvantages of syndication. In fact, in Chapter 3, I show that industry development plays a key role. Extension might show that a cohesive network is more important in Asian countries where collectivism is more pronounced. However, counter arguments might suggest that in competitive-individualistic markets such as the U. S. a close group of friends is more important. Future studies should fruitfully explore these questions.

Third, following previous VC literature, I looked at one measure of performance: exits, either through IPO or M&A. Although this practice is widely accepted in the VC literature, it is not without limitation for two reasons: (1) because it does not take into account the different incentives of the various actors. For example, the entrepreneur might be more interested in expanding the business, or in keeping the control of the company, rather than having a financial gain through an exit. On the other hand, some VCs might want an exit to gain track record, while others are more focused on the financial performance. Therefore, future studies might disentangle these performance effects; (2) other measure would hold different insights. For example, an interesting measure would be employment creation, or innovation, or market share. Future studies that are able to capture different types of measures could be able to theorize on the wider benefits of VC syndication.

Notwithstanding the limitations of each study on its own, I tried to offer a holistic picture of the benefits and costs of syndicates. The phenomenon of VC syndicates has received considerable attention but much remains to do. I hope that this research with its contributions, weaknesses, and peculiarities helps to develop the field further and inspire future, young (and less young) researchers, and to bring our knowledge even further. In the end, I believe that academia is about creating knowledge as much as communicating it and inspiring others to do the same. In the end, I hope I accomplished these goals.

Bibliography

Abell, P., & Nisar, T. M. 2007. Performance effects of venture capital firm networks. *Management Decision*, 45(5): 923–936.

Adler, P., & Kwon, S. 2002. Social capital: Prospects for a new concept. *Academy of Management Review*, 27(1): 17–40.

Ahuja, G. 2000. Collaboration networks, structural holes, and innovation: A longitudinal study. *Administrative Science Quarterly*, 45(3): 425–455.

Aiken, L. S., & West, S. G. 1991. *Multiple Regression: Testing and Interpreting Interactions*. Newbury Park, CA: Sage.

Aldrich, H. E., & Fiol, C. M. 1994. Fools rush in? The institutional context of industry creation. *Academy of Management Review*, 19: 645–670.

Aldrich, H., & Martinez, M. A. 2001. Many are called, but few are chosen: An evolutionary perspective for the study of entrepreneurship. *Entrepreneurship Theory and Practice*, 25(4): 41–56

Amit, R., Glosten, L. R., & Muller, E. 1990. Does venture capital foster the most promising entrepreneurial firms? *California Management Review*, 32(3):102–111.

Artz, K. W., & Brush, T. H. 2000. Asset specificity, uncertainty and relational norms: An examination of coordination costs in collaborative strategic alliances. *Journal of Economic Behavior and Organization*, 41: 337–362.

Avnimelech, G., & Teubal, M. 2006. Creating venture capital industries that co-evolve with high tech- Insights from an extended industry life cycle perspective of the Israeli experience. *Research Policy*, 35: 1477–1498.

Baden-Fuller, C., Ferriani, S., Mengoli, S., & Torlo, V. J. 2011. *The Dark Side of Alternative Asset Markets: Networks, Performance and Risk Taking*. Working paper.

Bae, J., & Gargiulo, M. 2004. Partner substitutability, alliance network structure, and firm profitability in the telecommunications industry. *Academy of Management Journal*, 47(6): 843–859.

Baker W. 1990. Market networks and corporate behavior. *American Journal of Sociology*, 96(3): 589–625.

Baltagi, B. H. 2008. *Econometric Analysis of Panel Data*. New York, NY: John Wiley & Sons.

Barden, J. Q., & Mitchell, W. 2007. Disentangling the influence of leader's relational embeddedness on interorganizational exchange. *Academy of Management Journal*, 50: 1440–1461.

Barringer, B. R., & Harrison, J. S. 2000. Walking a tightrope: Creating value through interorganizational relationships. *Journal of Management*, 26(3): 367–403.

Batjargal, B. 2003. Social capital and entrepreneurial performance in Russia: A longitudinal study. *Organization Studies*, 24: 535–556.

Battilana, J., & Casciaro, T. 2012. Change agents, networks, and institutions: A contingency theory of organizational change. *Academy of Management Journal*, 55(2): 381–398.

Baum, J. A. C. 1996. Organizational ecology. In S. Clegg, C. Hardy and W. Nord (eds.), *Handbook of Organization Studies*. London: Sage.

Baum, J. A. C., & Haveman, H. 1997. Love thy neighbor? Differentiation and agglomeration in the Manhattan hotel industry. *Administrative Science Quarterly*, 42: 304–338.

Baum, J. A. C., & Oliver, C. 1991. Institutional linkages and organizational mortality. *Administrative Science Quarterly*, 36: 187–218.

Baum, J. A. C., Calabrese, T., & Silverman, B. S. 2000. Don't go it alone: Alliance network composition and startups' performance in Canadian biotechnology. *Strategic Management Journal*, 21(3): 267–294.

Baum, J. A. C., McEvily, B., & Rowley, T. J. 2012. Better with age? Tie longevity and the performance implications of bridging and closure. *Organization Science*, 23(2): 529–546.

Beal, D. J., Cohen, R. R., Burke, M. J., & McLendon, C. L. 2003. Cohesion and performance in groups: A meta-analytic clarification of construct relations. *Journal of Applied Psychology*, 88(6): 989–1004.

Bell, G., Filatotchev, I., & Aguilera, R. 2014. Corporate governance and investors' perception of foreign IPO value: An institutional perspective. *Academy of Management Journal*, 57(1): 301–320.

Bellavitis, C., Filatotchev, I., & Kamuriwo, S. 2014. The effects of intra- and extra-industry networks on performance: A case of venture capital portfolio firms. *Managerial and Decision Economics,* 35(2): 129–144.

Bellavitis, C., Filatotchev, I., & Souitaris, V. 2017. The impact of investment networks on venture capital firm performance: A contingency framework. *British Journal of Management,* 28(1): 102–119.

Bellavitis, C., Filatotchev, I., Kamuriwo, D. S., & Vanacker, T. 2017. Entrepreneurial finance: new frontiers of research and practice: Editorial for the special issue Embracing entrepreneurial funding innovations. *Venture Capital: An International Journal of Entrepreneurial Finance,* 19(1–2): 1–16.

Bengtsson, O., & Hand, J. R. M. 2011. CEO compensation in venture-backed firms. *Journal of Business Venturing,* 26(4): 391–411.

Benjamin, B. A., & Podolny, J. M. 1999. Status, quality, and social order in the California wine industry. *Administrative Science Quarterly,* 44: 563–589.

Birley, S. 1985. The role of networks in the entrepreneurial process. *Journal of Business Venturing,* 1: 107–117.

Bonacich, P. 1987. Power and centrality: A family of measures. *American Journal of Sociology,* 92(5): 1170–1182.

Borgatti, S. P., Everett, M. G., & Freeman, L. C. 2002. *Ucinet for Windows: Software for Social Network Analysis.* Cambridge, MA: Analytic Technologies.

Brander, J. A., Amit, R., & Antweiler, W. 2002. Venture-capital syndication: Improved venture selection vs. the value-added hypothesis. *Journal of Economics & Management Strategy,* 11(3): 423–452.

Brass, D. J., Galaskiewicz, J., Greve, H. R., & Tsai, W. 2004. Taking stock of networks and organizations: A multilevel perspective. *Academy of Management Journal,* 47(6): 795–817.

Bruderl, J., & Preisendorfer, P. 1998. Network support and the success of newly founded businesses. *Small Business Economics,* 10: 213–225.

Burgers, W., Hill, C., & Kim, C. 1993. A theory of global strategic alliances: The case of the global auto industry. *Strategic Management Journal,* 14(6): 419–432.

Burt, R. S. 1992. *Structural Holes.* Cambridge, MA: Harvard University Press.

Burt, R. S. 2000. The network structure of social capital. In: Sutton, R. I., & Staw, B.M. (Eds.), *Research in Organizational Behavior*. Greenwich, CT: JAI Press.

Burt, R. S. 2001. Structural holes versus network closure as social capital. In N. Lin, K. S. Cook, & R.S. Burt (Eds.), *Social Capital: Theory and Research*, 31–56. New York, NY: Aldine de Gruyter.

Burt, R. S., & Knez, M. 1995. Kinds of third-party effects on trust. *Rationality and Society*, 7: 255–292.

Bygrave, W. D. 1987. Syndicated investments by venture capital firms: A networking perspective. *Journal of Business Venturing*, 2(2): 139–154.

Bygrave, W. D. 1988. The structure of the investment networks of venture capital firms. *Journal of Business Venturing*, 3: 137–157.

Bygrave, W. D., & Timmons, A. 1992. *Venture Capital at the Crossroads*. Boston, MA: Harvard Business School Press.

Casamatta, C., & Haritchabalet, C. 2007. Experience, screening and syndication in venture capital investments. *Journal of Financial Intermediation*, 16(3): 368–398.

Chaline, S., Arthurs, J. D., Filatotchev, I., & Hoskisson, R. E. 2012. The effects of venture capital syndicate diversity on earnings management and performance of IPOs in the US and UK: An institutional perspective. *Journal of Corporate Finance*, 18(1): 179–192.

Chiplin, B., Robbie, K., & Wright, M. 1997. The syndication of venture capital deals: Buy-outs and buy-ins. *Frontiers of Entrepreneurship Research*, 21(4): 9–19.

Christensen, C., & Raynor, M. 2003. *The Innovator's Solution: Creating and Sustaining Successful Growth*. Cambridge, MA: Harvard University Press.

Chung, S., Singh, H., & Lee, K., 2000. Complementarity, status similarity and social capital as drivers of alliance formation. *Strategic Management Journal*, 21(1): 1–22.

Cohen, W. M., & Levinthal, D. A. 1990. Absorptive capacity: A new perspective on learning and innovation. *Administrative Science Quarterly*, 35: 128–152.

Coleman, J. S. 1988. Social capital in the creation of human capital. *American Journal of Sociology*, 94: 95–120.

Combes, P. P., Lafourcade, M., & Mayer, T. 2005. The trade-creating effects of business and social networks: evidence from France. *Journal of International Economics*, 66(1): 1–29.

Companys, Y. E., & Mullen, J. S. 2007. Strategic entrepreneurs at work: The nature, discovery, and exploitation of entrepreneurial opportunities. *Small Business Economics*, 28: 301–322.

Cope, J. 2011. Entrepreneurial learning from failure: An interpretative phenomenological analysis. *Journal of Business Venturing*, 26(6): 604–623.

Cumming, D., & Dai, N. 2010. Local bias in venture capital investments. *Journal of Empirical Finance*, 17(3): 362–380.

Cumming, D. J., & MacIntosh, J. G. 2003. A cross-country comparison of full and partial venture capital exits. *Journal of Banking and Finance*, 27: 511–548.

Cumming, D. J., & MacIntosh, J. G. 2003. Canadian labor-sponsored venture capital corporations: Bane or boon? In A. Ginsberg & I. Hasan (Eds), *New Venture Investment: Choices and Consequences*, 169–200. Greenwich, CT: JAI Press.

Cumming, D. J., & Walz, U. 2010. Private equity returns and disclosure around the world. *Journal of International Business Studies*, 41(4): 727–754.

Cumming, D. J. 2006. The determinants of venture capital portfolio size: Empirical evidence. *Journal of Business*, 79(3): 1083–1126.

Cumming, D. J. 2007. Government policy towards entrepreneurial finance: Innovation investment funds. *Journal of Business Venturing*, 22(2): 193–235.

Cumming, D., Fleming, G., & Schwienbacher, A. 2006. Legality and venture capital exits. *Journal of Corporate Finance*, 12(2): 214–245.

Dahlander, L., & Frederiksen, L. 2011. The core and cosmopolitans: A relational view of innovation in user communities. *Organization Science*, 23(4): 988–1007.

De Clercq, D., Fried, V., Lehtonen, O., & Sapienza, H. J. 2006. An entrepreneur's guide to the venture capital galaxy. *Academy of Management Perspectives*, 20: 90 –112.

De Clercq, D., & Dimov, D. 2008. Internal knowledge development and external knowledge access in venture capital investment performance. *Journal of Management Studies*, 45(3), 585–612.

Dimov, D., & Milanov, H. 2010. The interplay of need and opportunity in venture capital investment syndication. *Journal of Business Venturing*, 25(4): 331–348.

Dimov, D. P., & De Clercq, D. 2006. Venture capital investment strategy and portfolio failure rate: A longitudinal study. *Entrepreneurship Theory and Practice*, 207–223.

Dionysiou, D. D., & Tsoukas, H. 2013. Understanding the (re)creation of routines from within: A symbolic interactionist perspective. *Academy of Management Review*, 38: 181–205.

Duysters, G. 1996. *The Dynamics of Technical Innovation: The Evolution and Development of Information Technology*. Cheltenham, United Kingdom: Edward Elgar.

Echols, A., & Tsai, W. 2005. Niche and performance: The moderating role of network embeddedness. *Strategic Management Journal*, 26: 219–238.

Enkel, E., & Gassmann, O. 2010. Creative imitation: Exploring the case of cross-industry innovation. *R&D Management*, 40(3): 256–270.

Ensley, M. D., Pearson, A. W., & Amason, A. C. 2002. Understanding the dynamics of new venture top management teams: Cohesion, conflict, and new venture performance. *Journal of Business Venturing*, 17(4): 365–386.

EVCA. 2010. *Pan European Private Equity and Venture Capital Activity.*

Faems, D., Janssens, M., & Neyens, I. 2012. Alliance portfolios and innovation performance connecting structural and managerial perspectives. *Group & Organization Management*, 37: 241–268.

Feldman, M. S., & Pentland, B. T. 2003. Reconceptualizing organizational routines as a source of flexibility and change. *Administrative Science Quarterly*, 48: 94–118.

Ferrary, M., & Granovetter, M. S. 2009. The role of venture capital firms in Silicon Valley's complex innovation network. *Economy and Society*, 38(2): 326–359.

Filatotchev, I., Wright, M., & Arberk, M. 2006. Venture capitalists, syndication and governance in initial public offerings. *Small Business Economics*, 26(4): 337–350.

Fombrun, C., & Shanley, M. 1990. What's in a name? Reputation building and corporate strategy. *Academy of Management Journal*, 33(2): 233–258.

Freeman, J., Carroll, G. R., & Hannan, M. T. 1983. The liability of newness: Age dependence in organizational death rates. *American Sociological Review*, 48(5): 692–710.

Freeman, L. C. 1977. A set of measures of centrality based on betweenness. *Sociometry*, 40: 35–40.

Fried, V. H., & Hisrich, R. D. 1995. The venture capitalist—a relationship investor. *California Management Review*, 37(2): 101–113.

Friedrich, R. 1982. In defense of multiplicative terms in multiple regression equations. *American Journal of Political Science*, 26: 797–833.

Fulghieri, P., & Sevilir, M. 2009. Size and focus of a venture capitalist' s portfolio. *Review of Financial Studies*, 22(11): 4643–4680.

Gabbay, S. M., & Zuckerman, E. W. 1998. Social capital and opportunity in corporate R&D: The contingent effect of contact density on mobility expectations. *Social Science Research*, 27: 189–217.

Galaskiewicz, J., & Shatin, D. 1981. Leadership and networking among neighborhood human service organizations. *Administrative Science Quarterly*, 26: 434–448.

Gao, G., Gopal, A., & Agarwal, R. 2010. Contingent effects of quality signaling: Evidence from the Indian offshore IT services industry. *Management Science*, 56(6): 1012–1029.

Gargiulo, M., & Benassi, M. 2000. Trapped in your own net? Network cohesion, structural holes, and the adaptation of social capital. *Organization Science*, 11(2): 183–196.

Geletkanycz, M. A., & Hambrick, D. C. 1997. The external ties of top executives: Implications for strategic choice and performance. *Administrative Science Quarterly*, 42(4): 654.

Gino, F., Argote, L., Miron-Spektor, E., & Todorova, G. 2010. First, get your feet wet. The effects of learning from direct and indirect experience on team creativity. *Organizational Behavior and Human Decision Processes*, 111: 102–115.

Goerzen, A. 2007. Alliance networks and firm performance: The impact of repeated partnerships. *Strategic Management Journal*, 28(5): 487–509.

Golden, P. A., & Dollinger, M. 1993. Cooperative alliances and competitive strategies in small manufacturing firms. *Entrepreneurship Theory and Practice*, 17: 43–43.

Gompers, P. A., & Lerner, J. 1999. An analysis of compensation in the US venture capital partnership. *Journal of Financial Economics*, 51: 3–44.

Gompers, P. A. 1995. Optimal investment, monitoring, and the staging of venture capital. *Journal of Finance*, 50(5): 1461–1489.

Gompers, P. A. 1996. Grandstanding in the venture capital industry. *Journal of Financial Economics*, 42(1): 133–156.

Gompers, P. A., Kovner, A., Lerner, J., & Scharfstein, D. 2008. Venture capital investment cycles: The impact of public markets. *Journal of Financial Economics*, 87(1): 1–23.

Gorman, M., & Sahlman, W. A. 1989. What do venture capitalists do? *Journal of Business Venturing*, 4: 231–248.

Granovetter, M. S. 1985. Economic action and social structure: A theory of embeddedness. *American Journal of Sociology*, 91: 481–510.

Greene, W. H. 2003. *Econometric Analysis.* Upper Saddle River, NJ: Prentice Hall.

Grewal, R., Lilien, G. L., & Mallapragada, G. 2006. Location, location, location: How network embeddedness affects project success in open source systems. *Management Science*, 52(7): 1043–1056.

Groh, A. P., Liechtenstein, H., & Lieser, K. 2013. *The Venture Capital and Private Equity Country Attractiveness Index 2013 Annual*. Barcelona, Spain: IESE Business School.

Gulati, R., & Gargiulo, M. 1999. Where do interorganizational networks come from? *American Journal of Sociology*, 104(5): 1439–1438.

Gulati, R., & Higgins, M. C. 2003. Which ties matter when? The contingent effects of interorganizational partnerships on IPO success. *Strategic Management Journal*, 24(2): 127–144.

Gulati, R. 1995a. Social structure and alliance formation patterns: A longitudinal analysis. *Administrative Science Quarterly*, 40(4): 619–652.

Gulati, R. 1995b. Does familiarity breed trust? The implications of repeated ties for contractual choice in alliances. *Academy of Management Journal*, 38(1): 85–112.

Gulati, R. 1999. Network location and learning: The influence of network resources and firm capabilities on alliance formation. *Strategic Management Journal*, 20: 397–420.

Gulati, R., Nohria, N., & Zaheer, A. 2000. Strategic networks. *Strategic Management Journal*, 21(3): 203–215.

Gulati, R., Sytch, M., & Tatarynowicz, A. 2012. The rise and fall of small worlds: Exploring the dynamics of social structure. *Organization Science*, 23(2): 449–471.

Gupta, A. K., & Sapienza, H. J. 1992. Determinants of venture capital firms' preferences regarding the industry diversity and geographic scope of their investments. *Journal of Business Venturing*, 7: 347– 362.

Hagedoorn, J., & Schakenraad, J. 1994. The effect of strategic technology alliances on company performance. *Strategic Management Journal*, 15: 291–309.

Hallen, B. 2008. The causes and consequences of the initial network positions of new organizations: From whom do entrepreneurs receive investments? *Administrative Science Quarterly*, 53: 685–718.

Hannan, M. T., & Freeman, J. H. 1984. Structural inertia and organizational change. *American Sociology Review*, 49: 149–164.

Hargadon, A. 2002. Brokering knowledge: Linking learning and innovation. In B. M. Staw & R. M. Kramer (Eds.), *Research in Organizational Behavior*, 24: 41–85. Greenwich, CT: JAI Press.

Hausman, J. A., & Taylor, W. E. 1981. Panel data and unobservable individual effects, *Econometrica*, 49: 1377–1398.

Hege, U., Palomino, F., & Schwienbacher, A. 2006, *Venture capital performance in Europe and the United States: A comparative analysis*, mimeo HEC.

Hite, J. 2005. Evolutionary processes and paths of relationally embedded network ties in emerging entrepreneurial firms. *Entrepreneurship Theory and Practice*, 29(1): 113–144.

Hite, J. M., & Hesterly, S. 2001. The evolution of firm networks from emergence to early growth of the firm. *Strategic Management Journal*, 22(3): 275–286.

Hochberg, Y. V., Ljungqvist, A., & Lu, Y. 2007. Whom you know matters: Venture capital networks and investment performance. *Journal of Finance*, 62(1): 251–301.

Hochberg, Y. V., Ljungqvist, A., & Lu, Y. 2010. Networking as a barrier to entry and the competitive supply of venture capital. *Journal of Finance*, 65(3): 829–859.

Hoffmann, W. 2007. Strategies for managing a portfolio of alliances. *Strategic Management Journal*, 28: 827– 856.

Hopp, C. 2009. When do venture capitalists collaborate? Evidence on the driving forces of venture capital syndication. *Small Business Economics*, 35(4): 417–431.

Hsu, D. H. 2004. What do entrepreneurs pay for venture capital affiliation? *Journal of Finance*, 59(4): 1805–1844.

Hsu, D. H. 2006. Venture capitalists and cooperative start-up commercialization strategy. *Management Science,* 52(2): 204–219.

IESE. 2010. *The Global Venture Capital and Private Equity Country Attractiveness Index*.

Jääskeläinen, M. 2012. Venture capital syndication: Synthesis and future directions. *International Journal of Management Reviews*, 14(4): 444–463.

Jääskeläinen, M., Maula, M. V. J., & Seppa, T. 2006. Allocation of attention to portfolio companies and the performance of venture capital firms. *Entrepreneurship Theory and Practice*, 185–206.

Jensen, M. C. 2003. The role of network resources in market entry: Commercial banks' entry into investment banking, 1991–1997. *Administrative Science Quarterly*, 48(3): 466–497.

Kale, P., Dyer, J. H., & Singh, H. 2002. Alliance capability, stock market response, and long term alliance success: The role of the alliance function. *Strategic Management Journal*, 23: 747–767.

Kaplan, S. N., & Schoar, A. 2005. Private equity returns: Persistence and capital flows. *Journal of Finance*, 60: 1791–1823.

Karlson, B., France, N. & Bellavitis, C. 2017 PowerbyProxi connecting the unknown dots in the commercialization of inductive power transfer. *Case Studies in Business and Management*, 4(2): 1–13.

Keller, R. 2001. Cross-functional project groups in research and new product development: Diversity, communications, job stress, and outcomes. *Academy of Management Journal*, 44(3): 547–555.

Kilduff, M., & Brass, D. J. 2010. Organizational social network research: Core ideas and key debates. *Academy of Management Annals*, 4(1): 317–357.

Knack, S., & Keefer, P. 1997. Does social capital have an economic payoff? A cross-country investigation. *Quarterly Journal of Economics*, 112(4): 1251–1288.

Kogut, B., Urso, P., & Walker, G. 2007. Emergent properties of a new financial market: American venture capital syndication, 1960–2005. *Management Science*, 53(7): 1181–1198.

Koka, B. R., Madhavan, R., & Prescott, J. E. 2006. The evolution of interfirm networks: Environmental effects on patterns of network change. *Academy of Management Review*, 31(3): 721–737.

Kotter, J. P. 1979. Managing external dependence. *Academy of Management Review*, 4(1): 87.

Kutner, M. H., Neter, J., Nachtsheim, C. J., & Wasserman, W. 2004. *Applied Linear Statistical Models* (4th ed.), Chicago, IL: McGraw-Hill/Irwin.

Labianca, G., Brass, D., & Gray, B. 1998. Social networks and perceptions of intergroup conflict: The role of negative relationships and third parties. *Academy of Management Journal*, 41(1): 55–67.

Lavie, D. 2006. The competitive advantage of interconnected firms: An extension of the resource-based view. *Academy of Management Review*, 31(3): 638–658.

Lee, C., Lee, K., & Pennings, J. M. 2001. Internal capabilities, external networks, and performance: A study on technology-based ventures. *Strategic Management Journal*, 22 (6–7): 615–640.

Lerner, J. 1994. The syndication of venture capital investments. *Financial Management*, 23(3): 16.

Lincoln, J. R., Gerlach, M. L., & Ahmadjian, C. L. 1996. Keiretsu networks and corporate performance in Japan. *American Sociological Review*, 61: 67–88.

Lindsey, L. 2008. Blurring firm boundaries: The role of venture capital in strategic alliances. *Journal of Finance*, 63(3): 1137–1168.

Lockett, A., Ucbasaran, D., & Butler, J. 2006. Opening up the investor-investee dyad: Syndicates, teams and networks. *Entrepreneurship Theory and Practice*, 30(2): 117–130.

Lorrain, F., & White, H. C. 1971. The structural equivalence of individuals in social networks. *Journal of Mathematical Sociology*, 1: 49–80.

Low, M. B., & Abrahamson, E. 1997. Movements, bandwagons, and clones: Industry evolution and the entrepreneurial process. *Journal of Business Venturing*, 12: 435–457.

Lubin, A. 1961. The interpretation of significant interaction. *Educational and Psychological Measurement*, 21(4): 807–817.

Ma, D., Rhee, M., & Yang, D. 2013. Power source mismatch and the effectiveness of interorganizational relations: The case of venture capital syndication. *Academy of Management Journal*, 56(3): 711–734.

Mäkelä, M. M., & Maula, M. V. J. 2006. Interorganizational commitment in syndicated cross-border venture capital investments. *Entrepreneurship Theory and Practice*, 273–298.

Manigart, S., & Wright, M. 2014. Venture capital investors and portfolio firms. *Foundations and Trends in Entrepreneurship*, 9(4–5): 365–570.

Manigart, S., Lockett, A., Meuleman, M., Wright, M., Landström, H., Bruining, H., Desbrieres, P., & Hommel, U. 2006. Venture capitalists' decision to syndicate. *Entrepreneurship Theory and Practice*, 30(2): 131–153.

Matusik, S. F., & Fitza, M. 2012. Diversification in the venture capital industry: Leveraging knowledge under uncertainty. *Strategic Management Journal*, 33(4): 407–426.

Maurer, I., & Ebers, M. 2006. Dynamics of social capital and their performance implications: Lessons from biotechnology start-ups. *Administrative Science Quarterly*, 51: 262–292.

McEvily, B., & Zaheer, A. 1999. Bridging ties: A source of firm heterogeneity in competitive capabilities. *Strategic Management Journal*, 20: 1133–1156.

McEvily, B., Jaffee, J., & Tortoriello, M. 2012. Not all bridging ties are equal: Network imprinting and firm growth in the Nashville legal industry, 1933–1978. *Organization Science*, 23(2): 547–563.

Megginson, W., & Weiss, K. 1991. Venture capitalist certification in initial public offerings. *Journal of Finance*, 46: 879–903.

Mehra, A., Dixon, A. L., Brass, D. J., & Robertson, B. 2006. The social network ties of group leaders: Implications for group performance and leadership reputation. *Organization Science*, 17: 64–79

Meuleman, M., Wright, M., Manigart, S., & Lockett, A. 2009. Private equity syndication: Agency costs, reputation and collaboration. *Journal of Business Finance and Accounting*, 36(5–6): 616–644.

Mizruchi, M. S., & Stearns, L. B. 2001. Getting deals done: The use of social networks in bank decision-making. *American Sociological Review*, 66: 647–671.

Murray, G. C. 1995. Evolution and change: An analysis of the first decade of the UK venture capital industry. *Journal of Business Finance and Accounting*, 22(8): 1077–1106.

Nahapiet, J., & Ghoshal, S. 1998. Social capital, intellectual capital, and the organizational advantage. *Academy of Management Review*, 23(2): 242–266.

Nahata, R. 2008. Venture capital reputation and investment performance. *Journal of Financial Economics*, 90(2): 127–151.

Oh, H., Chung, M. H., & Labianca, G. 2004. Group social capital and group effectiveness: The role of informal socializing ties. *Academy of Management Journal*, 47(6): 860–875.

Oh, H., Labianca, G., & Chung, M. 2006. A multilevel model of group social capital. *Academy of Management Review*, 31(3): 569–582.

Ostgaard, T. A., & Birley S. 1994. Personal networks and firm competitive strategy: A strategic or coincidental match? *Journal of Business Venturing*, 9(4): 281–305.

Ozmel, U., Reuer, J. J., & Gulati, R. 2013. Signals across multiple networks: How venture capital and alliance networks affect interorganizational collaboration. *Academy of Management Journal*, 56(3): 852–866.

Parkhe, A. 1993. Strategic alliance structuring: A game theoretic and transaction cost. *Academy of Management Journal*, 36: 794–830.

Payne, G. T., Moore, C. B., Griffis, S. E., & Autry, C. W. 2010. Multilevel challenges and opportunities in social capital research. *Journal of Management*, 37(2): 491–520.

Peng, M. W., & Luo, Y. 2000. Managerial ties and firm performance in a transition economy: The nature of a micro-macro link. *Academy of Management Journal*, 43(3): 486–501.

Penrose, E. 1959. *The Theory of the Growth of the Firm*. Oxford, United Kingdom: Basil Blackwell.

Perry-Smith, J. E., & Shalley, C. E. 2003. The social side of creativity: A static and dynamic social network perspective. *Academy of Management Review*, 28: 89–106.

Petty, J. S., & Gruber, M. 2011. "In pursuit of the real deal". A longitudinal study of VC decision making. *Journal of Business Venturing*, 26(2): 172–188.

Pfeffer, J., & Nowak, P. 1976. Joint ventures and interorganizational interdependence. *Administrative Science Quarterly*, 21: 398–419.

Pfeffer, J., & Salancik, G. R. 1978. *The External Control of Qrganizations*. New York, NY: Harper and Row.

Phalippou, L., & Gottschalg, O. 2009. The performance of private equity funds. *Review of Financial Studies*, 22(4): 1747–1776.

Phelps, C. C. 2010. A longitudinal study of the influence of alliance network structure and composition on firm exploratory innovation. *Academy of Management Journal*, 53(4): 890–913.

Podolny, J. M., & Baron, J. N. 1997. Resources and relationships: Social networks and mobility in the workplace. *American Sociological Review*, 62: 673–693.

Podolny, J. M. 1993. A status-based model of market competition. *American Journal of Sociology*, 98: 829–872.

Podolny, J. M. 1994. Market uncertainty and the social character of economic exchange. *Administrative Science Quarterly*, 39: 458–483.

Podolny, J. M. 2001. Networks as the pipes and prisms of the market. *American Journal of Sociology*, 107(1): 33–60.

Podolny, J. M. 2005 *Status Signals: A Sociological Study of Market Competition*. Princeton, NJ: Princeton University Press.

Pollock, T. G., Chen, G., Jackson, E. M., & Hambrick, D. C. 2010. How much prestige is enough? Assessing the value of multiple types of high-status affiliates for young firms. *Journal of Business Venturing*, 25(1): 6–23.

Powell, W. W., Koput, K. W., & Smith-Doerr, L. 1996. Interorganizational collaboration and the locus of innovation: Networks of learning in biotechnology. *Administrative Science Quarterly*, 41(1): 116–145.

Powell, W. W., White, D. R., Koput, K. W., & Owen-Smith, J. 2005. Network dynamics and field evolution: The growth of interorganizational collaboration in the life sciences. *American Journal of Sociology*, 110(4): 1132–1205.

Prahalad, C. K., & Hamel, G. 1990. The core competence of the corporation. *Harvard Business Review*, May–June: 79–91.

Provan, K. G., Fish, A., & Sydow, J. 2007. Interorganizational networks at the network level: A review of the empirical literature on whole networks. *Journal of Management*, 33(3): 479–516.

Reagans, R., & McEvily, B. 2003. Network structure and knowledge transfer: The effects of cohesion and range. *Administrative Science Quarterly*, 48(2): 240–267.

Reagans, R., & Zuckerman, E. W. 2001. Networks, diversity, and productivity: The social capital of corporate R&D teams. *Organization Science*, 12(4): 502–517.

Rider, C. 2009. Constraints on the control benefits of brokerage: A study of placement agents in U.S. venture capital fundraising. *Administrative Science Quarterly*, 54(4): 575–601.

Ring, P. S., & Van de Ven, A. 1994. Developmental processes of cooperative interorganizational relationships. *Academy of Management Review*, 19(1): 90–118.

Rosenkopf, L., & Nerkar, A. 2001. Beyond local search: Boundary-spanning, exploration, and impact in the optical disk industry. *Strategic Management Journal*, 22: 287–306.

Rowley, T., Behrens, D., & Krackhardt, D. 2000. Redundant governance structures: An analysis of structural and relational embeddedness in the steel and semiconductor industries. *Strategic Management Journal*, 21(3): 369–386.

Ruhnka, J. C., Feldman, H. D., & Dean, T. J. 1992. The "living dead" phenomenon in venture capital investments. *Journal of Business Venturing*, 7: 137–155.

Sapienza, H. J. 1992. When do venture capitalists add value? *Journal of Business Venturing*, 7: 9–27.

Sapienza, H., & Gupta, A. K. 1994. Impact on agency risk and task uncertainty on venture capitalists-CEO interaction. *Academy of Management Journal*, 37(6): 1618–1632.

Sapienza, H., Manigart, S., & Vermeir, W. 1996. Venture capital governance and value added in four countries. *Journal of Business Venturing*, 11(6): 439–469.

Saxenian, A. L. 1994. *Regional Advantage*. Cambridge, MA: Harvard University Press.

Semrau, T., & Werner, A. 2014. How exactly do network relationships pay off? The effects of network size and relationship quality on access to start-up resources. *Entrepreneurship Theory and Practice*, 38(3): 501–525.

Shapiro, D. L., Sheppard, B. H., & Cheraskin, L. 1992. In theory: Business on a handshake. *Negotiation Journal*, 8: 365–377.

Shipilov, A. V., & Li, S. X. 2008. Can you have your cake and eat it too? Structural holes' influence on status accumulation and market performance in collaborative networks. *Administrative Science Quarterly*, 53(1): 73–108.

Shipilov, A. V. 2006. Network strategies and performance of Canadian investment banks. *Academy of Management Journal*, 49(3): 590–604.

Shipilov, A. V. 2009. Firm scope experience, historic multimarket contact with partners, centrality, and the relationship between structural holes and performance. *Organization Science*, 20(1): 85–106.

Smith, R., Pedace, R., & Sathe, V. 2011. VC fund financial performance: The relative importance of IPO and M&A exits and exercise of abandonment options. *Financial Management*, 40(4), 1029–1065.

Soda, G., Usai, A., & Zaheer, A. 2004. Network memory: The influence of past and current networks on performance. *Academy of Management Journal*, 47(6): 893–906.

Song, W. 2004. Competition and coalition among underwriters: The decision to join a syndicate. *Journal of Finance*, 59(5): 2421–2444.

Sorenson, O., & Stuart, T. 2008. Bringing the context back in: The search for syndicate partners in venture capital investment networks. *Administrative Science Quarterly*, 53: 266–294.

Sorenson, O., & Stuart, T. E. 2001. Syndication networks and the spatial distribution of venture capital investments. *American Journal of Sociology*, 106(6): 1546–1588.

Stam, W., & Elfring, T. 2008. Entrepreneurial orientation and new venture performance: The moderating role of intra- and extra industry social capital. *Academy of Management Journal*, 51(1): 97–111.

Starr, J., & Macmillan, I. C. 1990. Resource cooptation via social contracting: Resource acquisition strategies for new ventures. *Strategic Management Journal*, 11: 79–92.

Steier, L., & Greenwood, R. 1995. Venture capitalist relationships in the venture structuring and post-investment stages of new firm creation. *Journal of Management Studies*, 32: 337–357.

Stewart, D. D., & Stasser, G. 1995. Expert role assignment and information sampling during collective recall and decision-making. *Journal of Personality and Social Psychology*, 69: 619–628.

Stuart, T. E., Hoang, H., & Hybels, R. C. 1999. Interorganizational endorsements and the performance of entrepreneurial ventures. *Administrative Science Quarterly*, 44(2): 315.

Suchman, M. C. 1995. Managing legitimacy: Strategic and institutional approaches. *Academy of Management Review*, 20: 571–610.

Tian, X. 2011. The role of venture capital syndication in value creation for entrepreneurial firms. *Review of Finance*, 16(1): 245–283.

Tiwana A. 2008. Do bridging ties complement strong ties? An empirical examination of alliance ambidexterity. *Strategic Management Journal*, 29(3): 251–272.

Tortoriello, M., Reagans, R., & McEvily, B. 2012. Bridging the knowledge gap: The influence of strong ties, network cohesion, and network range on the transfer of knowledge between organizational units. *Organization Science*, 23(4): 1024–1039.

Tsai, W. 2001. Knowledge transfer in intraorganizational networks: Effects of network position and absorptive capacity on business unit innovation and performance. *Academy of Management Journal*, 44(5): 996–1004.

Uzzi, B. 1996. The sources and consequences of embeddedness for the economic performance of organizations: The network effect. *American Sociological Review*, 61: 674–698.

Uzzi, B. 1997. Social structure and competition in interfirm networks: The paradox of embeddedness. *Administrative Science Quarterly*, 42: 35–67.

Venkataraman, N., Chi-Hyon, L., & Bala, I. 2008. Interconnect to win: The joint effects of business strategy and network positions on the performance of software firms. *Advances in Strategic Management*, 25: 391–424.

Venkatraman, N., & Chi-Hyon, L. 2004. Preferential linkage and network evolution: A conceptual model and empirical test in the U.S. video game sector. *Academy of Management Journal*, 47(6): 876–892.

Wasserman, S., & Faust, K. 1994. *Social Network Analysis: Methods and Applications*. Cambridge, United Kingdom: Cambridge University Press.

Wassmer, U. 2010. Alliance portfolios: A review and research agenda. *Journal of Management*, 36(1): 141–171.

Wiklund, J., Baker, T., & Shepherd, D. 2010. The age-effect of financial indicators as buffers against the liability of newness. *Journal of Business Venturing*, 25(4): 423–437.

Williamson, O. E. 1979. Transaction-cost economics: The governance of contractual relations. *Journal of Law and Economics*, 22: 233–261.

Wright, M., Gilligan, J., & Amess, K. 2009. The economic impact of private equity: What we know and what we would like to know. *Venture Capital*, 11(1): 1–21.

Wright, M., & Robbie, K. 1998. Venture capital and private equity: A review and synthesis. *Journal of Business and Accounting*, 25(5–6): 521–571.

Wright, M., & Lockett, A. 2003. The structure and management of alliances: Syndication in the venture capital industry. *Journal of Management Studies*, 40(8): 2073–2102.

Zaheer, A., & Venkatraman, N. 1995. Relational governance as an interorganizational strategy: An empirical test of the role of trust in economic exchange. *Strategic Management Journal*, 16: 373–392.

Zahra, S. 1996. Technology strategy and new venture performance: A study of corporate sponsored and independent biotechnology ventures. *Journal of Business Venturing*, 11: 289–321.

Zollo, M., Reuer, J., & Singh, H. 2002. Interorganizational routines and performance in strategic alliances. *Organization Science*, 13(6): 701–713.

Index

OTHER TITLES IN OUR FINANCE AND FINANCIAL MANAGEMENT COLLECTION

John A. Doukas, Old Dominion University, *Editor*

- *Rethinking Risk Management: Critically Examining Old Ideas and New Concepts* by Rick Nason
- *Towards a Safer World of Banking: Bank Regulation After the Subprime Crisis* by T.T. Ram Mohan
- *The Penny Share Millionaire: The Ultimate Guide to Trading* by Jacques Magliolo
- *Escape from the Central Bank Trap: How to Escape From the $20 Trillion Monetary Expansion Unharmed* by Daniel Lacalle
- *Applied International Finance Volume I, Second Edition: Managing Foreign Exchange Risk* by Thomas J. O'Brien
- *Tips & Tricks for Excel-Based Financial Modeling, Volume I: A Must for Engineers & Financial Analysts* by M.A. Mian
- *Tips & Tricks for Excel-Based Financial Modeling, Volume II: A Must for Engineers & Financial Analysts* by M.A. Mian
- *The Anti-Bubbles: Opportunities Heading into Lehman Squared and Gold's Perfect Storm* by Diego Parrilla
- *Applied International Finance Volume II, Second Edition: International Cost of Capital and Capital Budgeting* by Thomas J. O'Brien
- *Hypocrisy of the African Public Finance Management Framework: The Case of Malawi* by Kamudoni Nyasulu
- *Welcome to My Trading Room, Volume II: Basics to Trading Global Shares, Futures, and Forex: Create Your Own Brokerage* by Jacques Magliolo
- *Welcome to My Trading Room, Volume III: Basics to Trading Global Shares, Futures, and Forex—Advanced Methodologies and Strategies* by Jacques Magliolo
- *Enterprise Risk Management in a Nutshell* by Dennis Cox

Announcing the Business Expert Press Digital Library

Concise e-books business students need for classroom and research

This book can also be purchased in an e-book collection by your library as

- a one-time purchase,
- that is owned forever,
- allows for simultaneous readers,
- has no restrictions on printing, and
- can be downloaded as PDFs from within the library community.

Our digital library collections are a great solution to beat the rising cost of textbooks. E-books can be loaded into their course management systems or onto students' e-book readers.
The **Business Expert Press** digital libraries are very affordable, with no obligation to buy in future years. For more information, please visit **www.businessexpertpress.com/librarians.** To set up a trial in the United States, please email **sales@businessexpertpress.com.**

www.ingramcontent.com/pod-product-compliance
Lightning Source LLC
Chambersburg PA
CBHW062024200326
41519CB00017B/4922